David Batty's career spans more than 40 years of writing, producing, directing and shooting documentaries in Australia and, more recently, Papua New Guinea.

After moving with his son to Alice Springs in 1981, he helped establish the TV production unit at the Central Australian Aboriginal Media Association (CAAMA), where he made a vast array of films and videos, all of which were predominantly in Aboriginal languages and often made with or featuring pre-contact people.

Batty later moved with his wife and four children to Broome, where he teamed up with producer Jeni McMahon. There he wrote, shot and directed documentaries and TV series, including *Rodeo Road, Sisters, Pearls and Mission Girls, Jila, Desert Heart, Inventions from the Shed* and *Going Bush*. With a long history of making programs with and for Aboriginal people, he is well known for his multi-award-winning series *Bush Mechanics*, which he co-directed with Francis Jupurrurla Kelly.

Batty's recent projects include directing *Coniston*, the story of Australia's last massacre of Aboriginal people in central Australia; the web series *Black As*, which tracks four young men and their wild adventures across Arnhem Land; and the eight-part series *Truck Hunters* for Network 10, which follows the adventures of two men as they scour the countryside in search of old American trucks to restore to their former glory.

Batty lives off-grid on the New South Wales south coast, but heads north in winter.

BATTY'S BUSH BIBLE

HOW TO DO AUSTRALIA

TIPS, TRICKS & YARNS

DAVID BATTY

ABC
BOOKS

Aboriginal and Torres Strait Islander readers are advised

that this book contains images and names of people who have died.

 The ABC 'Wave' device is a trademark of the
Australian Broadcasting Corporation and is used
under licence by HarperCollins*Publishers* Australia.

HarperCollins*Publishers*
Australia • Brazil • Canada • France • Germany • Holland • India
Italy • Japan • Mexico • New Zealand • Poland • Spain • Sweden
Switzerland • United Kingdom • United States of America

HarperCollins acknowledges the Traditional Custodians
of the lands upon which we live and work, and pays respect
to Elders past and present.

First published on Gadigal Country in Australia in 2024
by HarperCollins*Publishers* Australia Pty Limited
ABN 36 009 913 517
harpercollins.com.au

A catalogue record for this book is available from the National Library of Australia

ISBN 978 0 7333 4334 6 (paperback)
ISBN 978 1 4607 1713 4 (ebook)

Cover design by HarperCollins Design Studio
Front cover image courtesy of the author; all other images by istockphoto.com
Internal design by Mietta Yans, HarperCollins Design Studio
Author photograph by Jen McMahon
Printed and bound in Australia by McPherson's Printing Group

Dedicated to my nature loving parents, John and Betty Batty,
and my first-born son, Chris, who left us way too early.

CONTENTS

1

Setting off with Dad and his bushwalking mates.

OUR BIG BACKYARD

Welcome to my humble tome

I've been going bush ever since I discovered my legs, and some of my earliest memories are of camping, canoeing, bushwalking and adventuring with my family on the New South Wales south coast. As a teen growing up in steel city Wollongong, I was also drawn to the bush as a place where we were free to chop down old British motorbikes and cars and bash them around the bush ... literally. As risky as it was, we always seemed to come home in one piece. This was my introduction to the wonderful world of all things mechanical.

In 1981, as a young single dad, I moved to Alice Springs and a whole new world presented itself, I hit the desert wide-eyed and ready for adventure. Little did I know how my mechanical past would become so prominent in my new life.

In no time I found myself immersed in the world of this country's first custodians, and I pursued my passion to create films and videos, especially for and with Aboriginal people. At that time, Aboriginal people were starting to gain autonomy amidst an array of fledgling organisations, one of which was the first Aboriginal radio station, CAAMA (Central Australian Aboriginal Media Association), which my brother had a fair hand in helping to create. Down the track I was asked to help establish its TV unit, and took on four Aboriginal trainees in the process. We started a video magazine-come-current-affairs show that was delivered every few months on video cassette throughout central Australia. Eventually, we got a remote commercial television service licence and established the first Indigenous satellite broadcasting service in Australia, called Imparja, an Arrernte word meaning footprint. The service now delivers mainstream programming throughout the Northern Territory and western New South Wales.

For 12 years I travelled extensively throughout the Northern Territory and northern South Australia, working with Aboriginal people to create a vast array of films and videos: documentaries, health promotions, film clips, children's films, land-rights videos – all predominantly in Aboriginal languages and often with pre-contact people.

When I moved to Broome in 1993 (by then I was married with four kids), I teamed up with producer Jeni McMahon to write, shoot and direct documentaries and TV series. My time in the Kimberley gave me a rare insight into the area and those who live and work there: the pearlers, stockmen, rodeo champs, singers, artists, dancers and keepers of the songlines.

With Jen at the Halls Creek Rodeo, Western Australia.

My work has taken me deep into Australia's lesser-known parts and to some of its most remote locations. Traversing deserts, meeting extraordinary characters, enduring breakdowns and hardships has been the making of a life I could never have imagined. Along the way I've travelled with wizened old men, hung out in Alice Springs with Arrernte locals and become lifelong mates with people like Warlpiri warrior Francis Jupurrurla Kelly, with whom I have made many films, including *Bush Mechanics*, himself a master of the ancient oral tradition of storytelling. His epic yarns about bush characters, massacres, survival and bush-mechanic feats would keep a fireside audience begging for more. Like all good storytellers, Francis never shied away from lashings of embellishment. On long trips out bush over days or even weeks, he'd keep us all in good spirits with his jokes and funny takes on just about everything.

Francis Kelly directing *Bush Mechanics*.

And of course, there's the conceptual world of ancient narratives that criss-cross the countryside, the Jukurrpa, or Dreamtime stories, with mythical characters, magical events, and songs and ceremonies that are central to them. My immersion into the world of this country's first custodians and their stories has brought on near-fatal laughing fits as well as deep sorrow and empathy.

 Watch Video: Making *Bush Mechanics*

All my films about or involving our Indigenous countrymen and women have been by invitation. I would like to thank them for trusting me and letting me into their lives *and* this vast playground we now call Australia. To live, travel and make films with the original inhabitants of central Australia, the Kimberley and Arnhem Land has been an absolute honour.

Shooting *Bush Mechanics*.

For me, the camera always feels like a huge audience sitting on my shoulder, sharing conversations and going to rarely seen places. And I've learnt and experienced enough to fill a library. Innovation, invention, making do with what you've got, keeping a car going no matter what, living from the land, deep ancestral knowledge of Country, ceremony and bush craft are just part of my life's curriculum from these incredible teachers.

My own story goes back six generations, being a direct descendant of convicts Mary Turner, who arrived on the First Fleet, and, serendipitously, David Batty, who arrived on the Third Fleet. Across the generations, my ancestors have been the first white folk to venture south of Sydney by land; were whipped to near death; survived Norfolk Island penal hell; captained trading ships in the Pacific; fossicked for gold; were among our first chemists and electricians; fought in wars; and had one of Sydney's first streets named after them – Batty Street in Balmain.

So, I can't help feeling I'm coming to you from a deeply connected place.

We are the stuff of stories, and I've had great storytelling mentors. As a child I listened to my grandfather's epic adventures in the bush and my mother's treasure chest of people, places and events, all embellished with glistening detail. I then perfected telling tales of my own to a captive audience during long drives, an evening by the fire, or from the swag.

Now, after more than 40 years of storytelling with a camera, it's time to put down the magic picture box, invest in a new word machine and commit to writing a book. I've always had a knack of defining, and finding an audience for, the 'believe it or not' yarns, characters and adventures that have punctuated my life's journey. So having some of it committed to print and sitting on bookshelves forever somehow makes me feel I've pushed the clock forward on my own mortality.

The information in this book is drawn from my personal experience, and I'm excited beyond words to be able to bring you snippets of bush know-how and personal anecdotes, and above all to encourage everyone to get out there and enjoy this incredible country. What you'll find in these pages is mirth, handy tips and some ripping yarns.

With my son Chris, Kings Canyon, Central Australia.

Camping with my daughter Gina, Tanami Track.

This book is *not* designed to be an exhaustive guide to all things camping, caravanning and motoring. If you do want detailed information on the pros, cons and costs of four-wheel drives, things you can tow, the best tents, recovery gear or dream destinations, there's plenty of information out there. Clubs, Facebook groups, the internet or the library can provide you with that.

Instead, my humble offering is a mix of helpful tips and hints learnt the hard way, along with plenty of yarns from a life off the beaten track, to inspire *you* to go bush, whatever that might mean to you.

I hope you enjoy *Batty's Bush Bible*.

FRANCIS JUPURRURLA KELLY – THE ORIGINAL BUSH MECHANIC

Francis Jupurrurla Kelly and I co-directed the TV series Bush Mechanics. *We've been close mates since the early 1980s and have made many films in the Warlpiri language together. Over the years, he has shown me around his Country and shared his knowledge of it. I owe a great deal to Francis.*

Our collaborative efforts in the creation of Bush Mechanics *and many other films provide insights into and recognition of the ingenious world of the Warlpiri, and show the outside world that this language and way of life are still going strong.*

Hopefully through this book you'll be inspired to get out there and discover new parts of this great big land and meet some of the locals like Francis, who have so much knowledge to share.

Francis speaks: As a boy I was good at sports. I used to win everything. Swimming, running and football. [The town of] Yuendumu was all right, real strict as it used to be run by the government at that time – welfare days. All the people used to earn their own living. The jobs were building and road maintenance, mechanic and carpenter. But in that time, there was only Welfare vehicles running around, no private. We didn't have cars – nothing – only vehicles like Land Rovers, Holden utes, Blitz and Bedfords.

Before television, before anything. In those days, the big job was stockman, because they're used to working in that area for the station owners. No telephone in that time. Radiotelephone only came in after.

Later I worked at the Yuendumu clinic. From there, I worked in the media job. It started from Telstra mob bringing all their gears in, like telephone and all that. And we decided: 'Ah, we should get media, too, and have our own.'

Old Darby [respected Elder] would say, 'We don't wanna lose our culture through this television. We will keep it strong or teach culture through our own television.'

Well in 1985 we went across to Kintore, and talked about medias, like people bringing in satellites and all that, and how were we going to cope with that because, you know, we were left behind. We want to teach our young people through that, now, today, I can see every community got their own media.

Aboriginal people wanted their own voice on the radio, and film making, that's why the CAAMA came along. It was Freda Glyn and Philip Batty they're the two that were working to make CAAMA and teach us, and David Batty, Jupurrurla, he was with us out in the field, getting all the stories together.

With Francis and Gordon while making Walrpiri *Sesame Street ... Manyu Wana.*

And he [David Batty] came out, and we made *Manyu Wana* (Warlpiri *Sesame Street*), and from there it got bigger and bigger. We started our own local TV with a transmitter, we had only VHS. Sometimes we used to go out and get stories from old people and put them on. What's really important is not losing language. But today we can put our language into a subtitle and people can read it.

Then Rachel Perkins rang up. She say: 'Hey, you have to compete each other for first filmmakers, you know.' I been ask David: 'Jupurrurla, we gotta go for that conference to put our story in.' They reckon: 'What Yuendumu mob gonna make?'

And me and him look at each other and we say: 'Bush Mechanics.'

Because we got no garage out in communities or out on the road, we can survive to fix our own motor car, and all that, you know, from our own skill, that's the idea we came up with, to show the world how we people survive on that.

And from there we made a little film and showed it to Rachel. Later we won that AFI award. It was good fun learning from each other: I learn from him, he learn from me, and we learn from the other boys with their ideas on the side. But they still wanted another one. When I went to Canberra one bloke said: 'Hey, we still want that Bush Mechanics to come back to life.'

Me and Francis having just won an AFI award for *Bush Mechanics*.

Well, we know each other pretty well because you know, he knows the skill, I know the skill, we've been sharing it, how to do it, you know, how to make proper films about Aboriginal people, and about the language, because he's got good sense of humour too in our society, David Batty, Jupurrurla, yeah, people gave him a skin name Jupurrurla, respect each other.

Every time, you know, like, people, when we were making film, young people used to go there, they wasn't slipping away doing other things, they had to stick with David, what he told them, or I told them, you know, they were alright, the young people, they enjoyed it.

We had to, you know, work out how to make these films suitable for people to watch, and all that, it was really hard, you're a film maker, you've got to go over and over again, talking to those people, the tribal people in that area, you've got to go back talk with that skin groups, and all that, because there's a little bit of complex in that area, that we can't film too, yeah.

We got same skin name's like, Jupurrurla to Jupurrurla, we are brothers, we respect each other, whatever he do, I help him, whatever I do, he help me, that's what it's meant to be about, you know, what family skin groups are.

Well, there's nothing secret between me and him, yeah. We joke, we tease each other, we work together. Sometimes he rings me up. If he can't ring me, that means he's flat out busy somewhere.

I didn't know much filmmaking, but he teach me and it all turns out... camera is a magic tool.

 Watch Video: Consiton Behind the Scenes

2

The Batty family camp, Araluen Valley, New South Wales.

SO YOU WANT TO GO BUSH

When I was a kid growing up in Wollongong, south of Sydney, we were forever hitting the road in the family Hillman Husky and then a 1966 VW Beetle with a trailer towing out back. Dad was a keen bushwalker and canoeist, so by the time I was a teen I'd travelled about, camping, bushwalking and canoeing rivers all over New South Wales.

When my brother got a job as an art teacher in the remote Aboriginal community of Papunya, a few hundred kilometres west of Alice Springs in the Northern Territory, long drives became a necessity. Well-engineered bitumen roads and highways were yet to come to remote Australia. The dreaded 'South Road' from Port

Augusta to Alice Springs was a dirt nightmare: potholes, endless corrugations and bulldust that ate cars was as good as it got. And after rain? Forget about it!

Broken shock absorber on the Old Stuart Highway, Northern Territory.

My first long drive to Alice was up the old dirt South Road when I was around 20 years old. The road was full of broken cars, crumpled wheel rims and the bones of many a chariot that just wasn't built for 1200 kilometres of hell.

Work on the brand-new bitumen Stuart Highway to Alice began in 1979, and by 1987 the job was done, and the era of broken axles, smashed windscreens, bent shockies and cars just giving up in the middle of nowhere was over. For better or worse, the bituminising fervour didn't extend to countless dirt roads and 'highways' that to this day present their fair share of challenges. But for many, that's what it's all about. To survive the Gibb, Tanami, Savannah Way, Plenty or Oodnadatta Track, to name a few, is still an achievement just short of pedalling a tricycle to the South Pole.

That said, going bush does not necessarily mean you're going to be *in* the bush, or even in a bushy place. It means you're going to less-populated areas away from your home environment – and there may be some actual bush involved. It might be a four-wheel-drive trip into the desert, exploring a tropical island, or a bushwalk through a national park. Even driving through small towns in rural Australia can be considered Going Bush.

If you're looking for a little more than lolling around on your banana lounge working through your book of sudoku puzzles, there are festivals and gatherings galore.

A BIT OF HISTORY ABOUT GOING BUSH

From the moment Europeans and other exotics arrived in the remote regions of Australia, they made inroads in all directions. Missionaries, telegraph-line construction crews, Afghan cameleers, pastoralists, soldiers, miners, dingo-scalp traders and a fair proportion of dodgy characters such as horse thieves and racketeers all ventured out to make their fortunes, steal land or save godless souls. Many never came back.

For a long time, camels that originally came with the Afghan cameleers to work on the overland telegraph were the preferred and only means of getting around. They were followed by horses, the odd pushbike, motorbikes, then Ford Model Ts and Blitz trucks.

Roadmaker Len Beadell's post and engraved plate marking the construction of the Gunbarrel Highway, Northern Territory.

By the 1950s, the legendary road maker Len Beadell and his crew were hard at it into the far-west regions of the Northern Territory and Western Australia under the employ of the weapons research establishment based at Woomera. They had the task of making roads to access the new rocket-testing and weather station at Giles in the Rawlinson Ranges. They pushed over to join the existing Canning Stock Route south from Sandy Blight Junction to Docker River and beyond.

Much of the exploration into the outback was done with mining in mind. Oil-exploration companies created roads to carry out seismic operations into the Gibson Desert and beyond. At the same time, various governments and churches established communities to cater for the influx of Aboriginal people who were either attracted to a new way of living or coerced into giving up their strong and ancient nomadic lifestyles to 'sit down longa one place'.

Over the past 45 years I've been privileged to hear many first-contact stories from people who were born in the bush, oblivious to the 20th century and the white-man's world. In the early 1980s, our home in Alice Springs became the unofficial HQ for friends who worked at the fledgling Aboriginal communities of Kintore and Kiwirrkurra just over the border in Western Australia, home to the Pintubi people. Most of the Pintubi mob over the age of 30 or so had their first encounters with white people in the 1960s, and some were still out there, yet to run into the 20th century.

A common thread in most of the first-contact stories is the first sighting of cars or the strange tracks they left behind.

Warlpiri man Jack Jakamarra spotted wheel tracks and thought they must have been made by some kind of monster. He followed them for days until he gave up. I've been told similar stories by other Pintubi,

Luritja, Warlpiri and Pitjantjatjara people. In fact, just about every older Aboriginal person I've interviewed or yarned with has a story about the first time they saw or rode in a car.

One of the earliest vehicles to be seen by our Warlpiri nomads was a 1935 18-hundredweight Chevrolet utility. It was owned by the indefatigable anthropologist, botanist and Aboriginal-rights activist Olive Pink. It's unclear if she drove it all the way up to her camp near the current Granites gold mine, but she conducted much of her field work in it. She took on the rough terrain with her assistants and guides, one of whom was my old Warlpiri mate Alec Wilson.

The Chevy broke down somewhere north of Cockatoo Creek on Anmatyerre Country, according to Alec, where it was abandoned and never seen again. Francis Jupurrurla Kelly has been on my back for decades to help him find it.

When to go

If you have the luxury of choosing what time of year to go bush, consider if you want to go when the rest of the country is doing the same thing – like school holidays, the Christmas/New Year period, or peak ski season – or whether you're in a position to go when things quieten down. School holiday time can be more fun if you've got a car full of kids, but expect to pay premium prices.

Another important factor is season and climate.

From around October to April it's wet season in north Australia. Having lived and worked in the north for much of my life, I've endured many a wet. Unless you particularly like high humidity, extreme heat, torrential rain, being cut off by floods or cyclones … go to your dream destination in the dry season.

In the wet, places like Broome become veritable ghost towns, with residents chasing air con from bedroom to car to work to shopping. The soupy oceans are unpleasant for swimming, due to sea lice and stingers, and too hot and choppy for fishing.

Check the area you want to visit but the dry is usually from around early May until September. Most festivals, events and fun times happen through June, July and August.

But when it comes to Victoria, Tasmania, the coast of South Australia, and south Western Australia, summer is the perfect time to go, while New South Wales is pretty good any time of the year, especially northern New South Wales.

For how long? Where to?

Whether you're bushwalking, caravanning or road tripping, there are some special places you may want to add to your go-to list, at least consider. The list below is mainly of out-of-the-way places or places to make a base and go exploring.

Where	What's on offer	When
West MacDonnell Ranges, Central Australia	Walking, camping, road trip	May–Aug
Bruny Island, Tasmania	Walking, camping	Nov–Apr
Broome, north-west WA	Beaches, historic town, festivals	May–Sept
Sapphire Coast, NSW south coast	Beaches, fishing, camping	Dec–May
Honeymoon Bay on Jervis Bay, NSW south coast	Camping, fishing, walks	All year
Winton, west Qld	Outback town, dinosaurs, festivals	May–Sept

Pretty Beach, NSW south coast	Camping, walking, swimming, fishing	All year
Brooms Head, NSW north coast	Camping, fishing, beaches	All year
Agnes Water, Far North Qld coast	Beaches, walks	All year
Hinchinbrook Island, Far North Qld	Bushwalking, camping, fishing	Mar–Sept
Tom Groggin, Snowy Mountains, NSW	Camping, river, fishing	Aug–May
Hamelin Bay, WA south coast	Camping, fishing, boating	All year
Litchfield National Park, NT	Camping, swimming, walks	Apr–Sept

ABORIGINAL LAND AND OTHER RESTRICTED AREAS

If you intend to visit or stay on Aboriginal land in places like Arnhem Land or the Central Desert areas, you may need to get a permit from the relevant Aboriginal land council. Do your homework and allow a fair window of time to get a response, or for your permit to come through. Visiting an Aboriginal community is usually by invitation. Some encourage visitors to fuel up and get supplies, but it's best not to go into an Aboriginal community unless you absolutely need to.

There are a few places in Australia that are totally off limits, due to defence operations. The Beecroft Peninsula, on the northern side of Jervis Bay on the south coast of New South Wales, is used by the Royal Australian Navy for target practice and is closed from time to time. It's best to check before you go so you aren't turned away at their boom gate.

Destination sorted

So you've thrashed out a destination with your inner adventurer or your partner and got approval from the kitchen-table committee. Looks like your old Hyundai may not make it to Cape York, you can't afford six weeks in Broome and the knees are going to let you down doing the Larapinta Trail in the West MacDonnells. Next momentous decision is what form of transport you will need and what you want to get horizontal in. Later in this book you'll find plenty of helpful info and some of my favourite and less-favourite journeys.

Resting at Bithry Inlet while bushwalking the New South Wales south coast.

BUSH BY FOOT

You don't always need wheels to enjoy a great adventure in our big backyard: exploring the wonderworld of what Mother Nature has provided for us can be done on foot. In Oz, we call it bushwalking.

The original owners of this huge continent had no option but to get around on foot. The nomadic tribes traversed massive distances, particularly in the arid regions. I have interviewed Pintubi, Warlpiri and Pitjantjatjara men and women who spoke of travelling on foot, carrying babies around their waists and lighting up the country with fire as they went to keep warm in winter months. They knew all the waterholes and rock holes (naturally formed pools of water) to sustain their long journeys, hunting along the way. Their motivation for long walks was to meet up with other family groups, to fulfil ceremonial obligations, or to find water. Or they might have been lone warriors on the hunt for a wife.

For our colonial forefathers, the bush was something to overcome and conquer. Fear it, clear it, burn it, plough it, fence it or get it productive with sheep, cattle and crops. Small chunks of land that were too difficult to farm or clear were left in their natural state. Luckily this usually meant the mountainous, remote or inhospitable places were left alone. The act of walking in the bush was not only an alien concept to these settlers, but frowned upon, and in some quarters seen as an 'ungodly' pursuit.

As the population swelled, and first and second generations of settlers and convicts now called Australia home, there was a growing sense of nationalism and a keenness to break away from the bonds of 'Mother England'. Poets, artists and writers began expressing a deep love and appreciation for the bush.

In the 1930s in Sydney, Myles Dunphy and a few of his nature-loving mates formed the Sydney Bushwalkers Club, of which my parents were both members.

Mum taking on a rock climb.

One of the club's first organised overnight bushwalks was into the Blue Mountains behind Sydney at the now famous (for some) Blue Gum Forest. This walk inspired a movement to protect it, and the conservation movement in Australia was born.

The idea that the bush and natural environments were something to protect and nurture caught on. The public began to demand that governments of the day be more proactive in conserving and protecting areas that might otherwise disappear under bulldozers. Ninety years on, and the Blue Gum Forest is at the heart of a larger national park and is World Heritage listed.

Both my parents caught the bushwalking bug early. Their courting days saw them don gear and head to the Blue Mountains, Snowy Mountains and Cradle Mountain in Tasmania. Throughout my childhood and teenage years, when we weren't doing a car camping trip, we'd head off with our gear and go bushwalking.

There was a hierarchy of canvas and leather packs (now referred to as backpacks or rucksacks), depending on the type of trip. The two-pocket pack was for day walks. The three-pocket pack was a little more serious and could fit more gear, but was heavier. The metal A-frame pack was for the serious few-day walks, while the H-frame pack was for the one-week walks and the truly devoted muscle-bound types. My brother and I had three-pocket packs, and Dad had the A-frame.

Camping along the Shoalhaven River.

Watch Video: Bushwalking South Coast

Our bushwalking tents were lightweight two-man A-types made of japara or waxed cotton, and with no floor and no walls. But they had the fabulous ability to be 'abdulled': this meant one side of the tent could be lifted and tied to nearby trees to make shade for a lazy afternoon by a river or beach. Most of our other gear was from Dad's early bushwalking days, that is, no plastic: aluminium containers for tea and powdered milk, homemade aluminium billies, an oilskin ground sheet, non-zippered sleeping bags – you get the idea.

From about the age of eight I was ready to take on serious bushwalks with my brother and father. After Dad had finished work at Port Kembla on a Friday, Mum would drop us off and we'd head off into the night. We especially loved the Budawangs, a wild set of sandstone mountains, valleys and sheer cliffs rising out of the forest and defined by the meanderings of the Clyde River west of Batemans Bay on the New South Wales south coast. At the time, I prided myself on being the first and youngest white kid to climb the spectacular peaks of mountains like the Castle, Mount Tarn and Currockbilly and to wander through the surreal Monolith Valley.

Apart from the challenge of rock climbing, genuine bush bashing and the glory of reaching spectacular peaks, I loved camping in the caves. This meant we never had to carry tents; rather, we'd cut some bracken and set it out on bare rock, throw down our oilskin ground sheet over the top, roll out our sleeping bags and call it our bed for the night. It was always dry and the rock ceiling reflected the flickering fire nearby. Caves were also favoured by bush rats and wallabies, which would often visit throughout the night.

Cave camping, Monolith Valley, Budawang Ranges.

Other destinations and longer five-day or one-week walks took us to the Snowy Mountains to climb Mount Jagungal and its neighbouring peaks. The Blue Mountains was another fave with walks around Kanangra Walls, through the Wild Dog Mountains and down to the Coxs River. But the walk that's stayed with me to the point that I can recount it in detail is the week we spent on the Shoalhaven River near Bundanoon in New South Wales.

Our walk down to the mighty gorges of the Shoalhaven started from the Long Point Track lookout near Tallong, a tiny farming outpost, and the view is all down. From up high the Shoalhaven

Preparing breakfast, Budawang Ranges.

resembles a fine ribbon of water meandering through near-vertical hills and peaks, as it cuts its way from Braidwood to Nowra near the coast. The walk to Louise Lake has your knees trembling and thighs in agony, but a great lakeside camp awaits. I remember catching fat and slimy eels, cooking them in the coals and serving them with lightly boiled fresh stinging nettle, which luckily loses its sting after cooking.

My brother Philip and I looking out over the Budawang Ranges from The Castle.

A riverside track takes you to places like Bungonia Gorge with boulders as big as houses, the Block Up, where the river snakes through a rock-walled crack in the mountains, and an abandoned silver mine with a chimney so high you can see stars if you look up it. Lazing around by the river or lake in our abdulled tent with Dad's walking mates and a pack of cards, I soon became pretty stiff competition in whist, solo, five hundred and eventually bridge.

My days of bushwalking as a child formed part of who I am today and instilled in me the desire to continue the practice. As a young dad I'd carry my firstborn in a papoose with a pack on my back and camp in caves and beaches in the Royal National Park south of Sydney (which is still a magnificent place to visit). My time building a family in Alice Springs saw major expeditions along the West and East MacDonnell Ranges, a must-do for any outdoor enthusiast. And over the past 20 years, I've done countless three- to five-day walks along the New South Wales south coast, as well as more benign walks camping by pristine beaches, rivers and estuaries. These are now my go-to places where we can swim, dive for and eat abalone, fish and loll about on lawns kept low by grazing kangaroos.

Thanks, Dad.

 Watch Video: Snowy River - first time canoed

3

Me and my son Chris in Alice Springs.

WHEELS AND SHELTER

In January 1981 I hit the road with my five-year-old son in a Holden panel van, otherwise known as a shaggin' wagon. They were the number-one choice for surfers who would deck them out with shag-pile carpet, eight-track stereos and a mattress ... thus the name. Mine was a little more sedate. This time we drove from Wollongong to Alice via Queensland. The van had the ubiquitous mattress in the back, which was our all-weather sleeping arrangement. It was wet season, and every overflowing river from Emerald to Mount Isa had cut the road into short chunks of drivable bitumen between stretches of water. Back then four-wheel drive vehicles were less common, so taking on inundated roads was out of the question. Cars and their passengers had no option but to sit tight on their strip of road surrounded by brown floodwater for hours and sometimes days. A fellow strandee in a milk tanker was handing out buckets of fresh milk to keep the line of travellers nourished. Eventually the rivers dropped and the cavalcade of strandees could move on to. We arrived in Alice with all our worldly possessions in or on the van, which didn't amount to much. The Holden didn't miss a beat, and delivered Chris and me to our new home, ready to start a whole new chapter.

My trusty Datsun 1500 that never gave up.

While the highway we took has since been improved out of sight with causeways and bridges, the experience instilled in me a sense of 'anything can happen at any time when you're on the road' – and encouraged me to always be prepared!

Wheels

The guiding principle and intention of this book is not to preach a preferred means of getting about, but to encourage you to go bush and enjoy our big backyard any way you can. Motorbikes, cars, motorhomes, caravans, trailers – they all add up to the same thing, which is that first step on the road to adventure. Any kind of vehicle with wheels and a propulsion device can get you out there. Just ask any bush mechanic (more about them later), who's usually not fussed about which vehicle, so long as it keeps going to where you want to get to. You can even sleep in a car once you've done your circus training as a contortionist.

How you decide on your set of wheels will be determined by the kind of places you want to explore, your budget and the level of comfort you're after.

Here's a quick rundown on the options out there and some of the things you'll need to consider before you say goodbye to suburbia and float off down the bitumen river on your dream holiday.

Travelling couple who have lapped Australia several times, Kimberley.

Tanami Track camp with Clayton.

Car/wagon

Normal, everyday cars and wagons, whether they be two-wheel drive (2WD), all-wheel drive (AWD) or four-wheel drive (4WD), will get you to where you want to go (depending on road conditions) – just ask any backpacker. Sleeping inside one is fine, especially if it's a wagon, but a normal sedan … you would be better off sleeping in a wheely bin. If it's your only option, get a tent and look out for public barbecues or a picnic shelter where you can cook on a portable gas cooker. Failing this, pretend you're bushwalking and make camp.

If you want to hitch a caravan or trailer on the back, you'll need a few extra horses under the bonnet, so a four-wheel drive is highly recommended. Check the weight of what you'll be hitching to, and the towing capacity and ball weight of your towing machine – *and* what your insurance policy will allow.

Ute

Many of us, including myself, just want to keep it simple: load up the essentials and head off. A ute with a canopy and roof racks on both or either can carry all your camping gear, but will usually mean you'll be getting horizontal in a tent or swag and cooking on the fire or tailgate. This mode suits me perfectly.

ADDITIONAL DRIVING LIGHTS

If you expect to be cruising country roads at night, driving lights are an essential item, unless your travelling machine comes with extra superior day-making beams, which hardly any do.

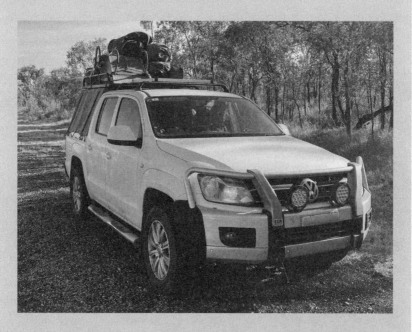

The question is which lights to get. There are arguments for all types along the lines of distance, reach, spread, colour temperature, lux, glare, eye strain, light bar or round type – LED, HID (high-intensity discharge) or halogen – and size.

What you choose will probably come down to what your wallet and the front of your chariot can handle. I've found a combination of light bar and two LED spotlights do the job. Halogens have replaceable bulbs and are said to be less strain on your eyes. Do your online research because there are hundreds of options. But lighting up the road ahead might just save your life.

Twin cab or SUV

Both the good ol' twin cab and the SUV are perfectly good for a long trip or a bit of local camping. Being four-wheel drive they'll get you even deeper into adventure land and out-of-the-way places. You're unattached and free.

The mighty EJ Holden as seen in *Bush Mechanics*.

SOME BUSH CARS I HAVE KNOWN

When I was shooting the TV show *Bush Mechanics* about young men in cars near Yuendumu on Warlpiri Country in the Northern Territory, I came across some incredible bush chariots. A clapped-out car in the bush presents endless opportunities to teach mechanical knowledge and ingenuity, as well as the joys of bush bashing.

Each car has a unique story worth telling. Some have ended up a pile of burnt and twisted metal in the scrapheap; others have gone on to be showcased in travelling exhibitions or have survived every kind of abuse and are still going today.

Not all the cars that make an appearance are mentioned here, just the ones that drive a good story.

The 1974 Holden Statesman De Ville - the car that didn't make it

The *Bush Mechanics* budget was so meagre that buying a decent, running car was way out of the question. Luckily (or more to the point, unluckily), I clapped eyes on a 1974 Holden Statesman De Ville in disrepair and abandoned on the outskirts of the community. The De Ville represents the peak

The Holden Statesman De Ville thrashed and left for dead.

of General Motors engineering, luxury, power and cool seventies style. It came standard with a 308 V8 power plant, automatic gearbox, fully reclining seats, electric windows – the works.

I tracked down the car's owner, who said it was all mine, so I had it towed to my accommodation. Upon further inspection it was perfect for the job: lots of room inside for filming, authentically trashed from hunting and firewood collecting, and with upholstery that was fully mulched by scores of sweaty bodies, kangaroo blood and greasy takeaway food.

But getting it going proved to be a challenge greater than winning the Finke Desert Race. The motor resisted all attempts at resuscitation. Water pouring out of what remained of the head gasket was a sure sign it had been run dry to the point it buckled the head, leaving a gap you could throw a boomerang through.

I eventually pulled both heads off the V8 and bailed out the pools of water wallowing around in the block, bolted and glued what remained of the head gaskets on with several tubes of gasket goo and silastic. I jumped the battery, twisted the ignition wires together, earthed the starter solenoid with the dipstick – and bingo! It was purring like eight kittens in a wicker basket.

While all eight cylinders were merrily firing away, emitting barely visible packets of steam, I felt confident the old legend could do with a lap of the community. I felt like royalty, receiving waves and cheers from the locals, who were super pleased to see the good ol' hunting car back on the road. Then it stopped. Right out the front of the community store – for good. With clouds of steam still billowing from under the crumpled bonnet, it was towed to its final resting place, back at the very spot I first saw it.

Time to look for another car.

The Holden Commodore VK – the Bush Basher

Having given up on the Statesman De Ville, I approached the owner of another vehicle that fitted the bill: a 1984 Holden Commodore VK. It was a fairly pedestrian, no-nonsense car that populated most suburbs throughout Australia. This particular specimen, however, had no wheels and no windscreen, but the interior was suitably mulched, making it a good fit for the show.

I approached the owner, who I'd known for some years. She said it was her favourite car and a good one, because a year earlier it had been running. I could have it cheap – $3500! Once I realised she wasn't joking, I was left with few options. Back then, any car was seen as an asset, as Yuendumu was a remote community with car-destroying roads leading to it and from it – and cars didn't grow on trees.

I went with the price, then went looking for wheels. Brand new ones were way out of the question, price-wise and availability-wise, and just an altogether unwise choice for a bush basher.

I wandered about the community, on the hunt for the right-sized wheels with tyres.

I found a wheel out the front of a corrugated-iron igloo. The tyre was flat and the treads worn down to the wire. On top of this, the wheel-stud holes were worn to the size of golf balls.

I approached the occupant of the humpy, the obvious owner.

'Nah, Jupurrurla, that's my favourite one. It got me from Nyirripi, right up to here.'

'But it's completely worn out.'

'Sorry, Jupurrurla, you can't have it.'

Clearly the wheel had earned lasting respect for the hard yards it had put in over its long, bumpy life. It had been on one hell of a journey, carrying several cars' worth of occupants long distances and withstanding millions of kilometres of dodging mulga stakes and punishing corrugations. Now it would sit in pride of place out the front of a corrugated iron humpy for eternity, left alone in its deflating years to ponder what vehicular life is wheely about.

So, I had to move on. I eventually scoured the dump and borrowed some wheels I found there with the promise of returning the bald and buckled old things to the owners once we finished filming. To be discarded meant they were in bad shape – an understatement, since they had stud holes you could drive through and exposed wire. Attaching them to the VK called for serious bush mechanics, muscle and a heavy hammer.

Despite enduring a punishing shoot, the VK soldiered on, bulldozing through mulga scrub, churning through deep sand, hitting sump-destroying boulders, earning flat tyres and a flat battery and ending up with a dead petrol pump, requiring the petrol be bypassed via the windscreen-washer pump. But it just kept going, even when the automatic transmission oil bailed out and the only gear left that worked was reverse. It just wanted to live, no matter what.

Its time was up when the transmission finally called it a day. It begged to be left alone to make peace with its Holden makers in the sky, and finally became one with its spinifex and mulga surrounds.

The 1964 Holden EJ Dragin Wagin

After a gap of a few years and the overwhelming success of the first *Bush Mechanics* one-off half hour on the ABC, I arrived in Yuendumu ready to take on a four-part series. My co-director (and now *Bush Mechanics* star) Francis Jupurrurla Kelly had procured a baby-blue 1964 Holden EJ station wagon in pretty good shape – apart from having zero brakes, missing doors, a worn-out motor and suspension that wouldn't suspend a wet paper bag.

It was perfect.

The EJ performed magnificently in the lead-up to its endurance test: a drive with a car full of grown men with enough band gear on the roof to fill a road train, including speaker bins that would deafen a crowd at the MCG. The baby-blue cargo ship of the desert was rocking and rolling along nicely – until the roof caved in. Undeterred, the boys removed the band gear, chopped the roof off, tied it to the back of the wagon, put the gear on the roof and used it as a sled. This slowed down the poor old pensioner EJ, which should have been retired to a museum years before. Old baby-blue was crying clouds of smoke and down to its last two firing cylinders when we decided it was time to call in a support vehicle and towed the poor old thing the last 20 or 30 kilometres. (Besides, it was getting dark, and the EJ's headlights had given up back in the 1960s.)

After filming, the EJ ended up in Francis's front yard. It wasn't there long before a *Bush Mechanics* devotee at the National Museum in Canberra could see it was worthy of a whole new life at the museum. Consequently, Francis scored some dolla and it was trucked down to enjoy its retirement at the nation's capital. But not for long. A few years later, it was part of a touring *Bush Mechanics* exhibition, which is still on the road today.

Popular free camp amidst the Oscar Ranges, Kimberley, Western Australia.

Shelter

When it comes to getting horizontal after a long day, some are comfortable stretching out on nothing but Mother Earth, like the hardened Kimberley stockman Johnny James. When the cattle were yarded up and the sun had given up for the day he'd think nothing of stretching out next to a stockyard in thick trammelled bulldust with a cow pat for a pillow. But most of us like a little comfort, and for me that's the good ol' swag. Real swags (more on that later) provide front-row seats to the stars and the company of a warm flickering campfire. Come rain, mozzies and cold winds, though, it's nice to have something between you and the outside world. This might be in the form of a tent or something with wheels.

Typical bushwalking camp along the New South Wales south coast.

Tent

Don't get me wrong about tents. I like my swag, but tents are a great way to go as well. There are too many sizes, types and variations to list here but being a tent buyer, inhabitant, carrier and sharer, I've arrived at a few likes, dislikes and things to take into consideration.

The two-person walking tent.

Hike tent

As the name suggests a hike tent is for hiking – or, as we call it in Australia, bushwalking. When I was a child growing up in a keen bushwalking family, our tent was a Paddy Pallin japara (waxed cotton) A-frame tent with no floor or walls. If you touched the sides of the tent when it was raining, it would start an indoor stream or a persistent drip onto your sleeping bag. The upside was these tents breathed easily, were lightweight and you could 'abdul' one side and create a shady place to relax through the day.

Hike tents have to be small enough to roll up and fit into a backpack along with your sleeping mat, sleeping bag, food, utensils and whatever else you need to walk, camp and sleep in relative comfort and stay dry. So, weight is a critical factor when you're about to commit to owning or borrowing one, and weight is directly related to the size.

Tents seems to be universally measured in 'persons': one-person, two-person, three-person, 12-person, far more politically correct than the previous 'man' sizing. I've found this measure to be unreliable or ambitious to say the least—and not because of gender. To share a two-person tent with someone you are intimately familiar with is one thing, but to share it as two autonomous stand-alone individuals is another.

But the more 'persons' a tent is designed for, the heavier it gets. A lightweight two-person tent is considered to be around 2–3.5 kilograms, while a one-person equivalent can get down to 800 grams. Hike tents are mostly a dome style made from polyester or nylon, with fibreglass or aluminium rods, built-in floor, zip-up insect-proof netting and a fly that goes over the top to keep the weather out.

PEG IT RIGHT, KEEP IT TIGHT

When erecting your temporary overnight (or longer) accommodation, it's important to firstly peg out the floor nice and tight to make it leakproof and as secure as the grip on your stubby. Then peg down your fly and guy ropes firmly so your sleeping temple does not succumb to collapse in the event of cyclonic conditions outside.

Rooftop tent

For anyone who doesn't mind the confines of a two-person tent, especially those who like their romantic prospects in a small rooftop dwelling, rooftop tents are the go. They've become a thing, and every second four-wheel drive not towing something seems to have one.

From personal experience, I've found getting your sleeping arrangements off the ground and up in the air is particularly handy in crocodile and snake country. I've always had heavy-duty roof racks with a sturdy mesh floor to use as a filming platform. If I found myself in the company of Joey Blakes (snakes) or large slithering lizards, I'd roll my swag out up high. Croc country can also be hot and sticky, so being elevated also means catching a breeze.

As an alternative to a camper trailer or van, rooftop tents are way cheaper and can go to whatever private paradise your four wheels can get you to. You can slip one on when you're ready to hit the road and take it off when you're back home and back to the humdrum of normality. They're priced from under a grand to two to three grand, and you can choose from a multitude of options: soft-top, hard-shell, a variety of storage space, more or fewer windows and flaps – and then there's the ladder. A disadvantage for some may be the telltale rocking from close interpersonal interactions, which may also be an advantage.

You'll need to be able-bodied and have a strong bladder and some decent roof real estate or tray-top space. Whichever way you go, they all share the same pros:

- ready-made comfy bed
- easy to set up and take down
- views
- breeze
- away from bugs and crawlies

MARTY AND JACK

Rooftop campers

Edith River near Katherine, Northern Territory

On a recent drive through the Northern Territory, I ran into a young couple who were camped by the Edith River near Katherine. They'd come up through central Australia all the way from Jervis Bay on the south coast of New South Wales.

'We're doing a lap around Australia,' Marty said, 'including a six-month drive around the top of WA, then heading down the WA coast and across South Australia and Victoria to home.'

Along the way, they were planning to look for some work. 'Well, I'm an electrician,' Jack said, 'and Marty is an outdoor guide. So we're looking to get a bit of work to fund the back half of the trip.'

Their rig, a 2005 HiLux single cab, was super impressive, and they looked totally sorted. Jack did most of the work himself, including the tray build, the canopy fit and a lot of the interior. 'We've got the full canopy set-up, rooftop tent and suspension lift, tyres, winch and bar work. All the stuff to make it capable.'

Marty and Jack had chosen the rooftop tent for several reasons.

'One, it's a lot cheaper, and two, we can go anywhere we want to,' Jack said. 'We're not towing anything, so we can go down any four-wheel-drive track and easily and quickly set up in under a minute and pack up in under a minute. That's pretty awesome.'

I asked them how they found sleeping on the roof.

'It's quite comfy,' Marty said. 'You're not sleeping on rocks, you're up out of the way, and it's nice in the hot weather as you get a bit of breeze. There's lights and chargers up there, which are quite handy. You can sit up and play games and watch movies on your phone.'

Marty and Jack used word-of-mouth and camping apps to find camping spots. Their favourite spot so far was a beach camp at Dundee Beach near Darwin. 'We were set up looking straight out into the water and had the sunset over the water,' Marty said. 'It was pretty awesome.' I asked them if they often found a little out-of-the-way spot to have to themselves.

'Yeah, we like pretty quiet camping,' Marty said. 'We like a bit of space between us and the next people. We don't like the sort of commercialised spots so much. And we definitely like free camping. Caravan parks don't really interest us.'

It sounded like this trip would not be their last. 'We've got lots more trips planned around Oz,' Jack declared.

Overnight travelling tent and drying our wet bedding at Cactus, South Australia.

Travelling tent

If you're not carrying your temporary accommodation around on your back, on the roof, or strapped to the petrol tank of your motorbike, but have a car to carry it for you, the choices are endless. A travelling tent is one that can be pulled from the boot or roof rack, erected quickly and easily, and accommodate a small group of people, often referred to as a 'family'. Tunnel, geodesic, pop-up, three-person, six-person, polyester or canvas – there are camping shops full of options. My all-time-favourite, no-fuss, quick-and-easy variety is the canvas centre-pole tent. Peg out its four corners, lift the roof up with just one telescopic tent pole and say goodbye to the expensive family room at the next roadside motel. Being canvas, it can last a few decades if packed away dry. The centre-pole tent comes with robust zips and roll-up windows, and can sleep two comfortably either side of the pole, four people who don't mind a bit of spooning, or a family of up to six, if the kids like pretending they're sardines. This is how my family of six stayed dry when we weren't in swags on scores of trips from Alice or Broome to all corners of the continent. We loved it (when not in the path of a tropical cyclone! ... but that's another story).

Long-stay tent

If you've found your dream destination, idyllic beach or river, or you're camping at your relative's place for the school holidays, a large tent will make your stay super comfortable and allow you to buy all the accessories known to camping. Just visit any crowded camping ground by any beachside or lake to see the elaborate set-ups and homes away from home. These camps are not for the nomads who like to burn rubber cross-country, emerging from their packed vehicular cocoons for a swim, coffee or op-shop bargain before zooming off to the next Ye Olde town for a steak sandwich. They're for the serious long-stayers: a week at least.

Long-stay tents can be made from a variety of fabrics, such as canvas, nylon, polyester or polyurethane. There are pros and cons with all of them, but my money is on canvas, which makes for a more robust and long-lasting option.

All varieties come in enough shapes, sizes and rooms to fill an IKEA catalogue. It might be a good idea to invest in a few jars of logic pills or do a crash course in pole identification, because there will be more poles than a salami shop in Warsaw. When I was camping at a popular New South Wales camping ground I noticed that most of the long-termers had erected huge blue plastic tarps with their own poles over the entire tent set-up. I can only guess this was for extra rain and sun protection, and, more than likely, to make the tent last longer.

Blow-up tent

The latest in outdoor sleeping accommodation is the blow-up or air tent. Their makers claim they are super robust in wind and better at keeping out the weather, and they do away with poles, which is a major breakthrough in setting up. The downside is they cost more, are heavier and a puncture or burn hole would be particularly deflating. You also need a pump.

Bell tent

The conical centre-pole bell tent has been around since the 1850s. A US army officer had one made based on his observations of a traditional First Nations American teepee but without the hole in the top for emitting smoke. This is probably why they're so popular in places like northern New South Wales or anywhere else where communities of young folk like to gather and live out their nomadic fantasies. They are super spacious inside, with flaps that let in fresh air, or you can roll up all the walls and it becomes a giant floating umbrella.

To date I have had four of these tents at my bush block. They come in cotton, poly-cotton or straight polyester. They make for great semi-permanent accommodation when extra guests arrive, and they look really cool. You'll need to allow half a day to erect one, and plenty of patience. It's also advisable to take them down when not in use as they are particularly prone to mildew – I've had to throw out two due to mildew infestation.

Glamping

This is a clever pursuit that evokes images of luxurious glamour while running the gauntlet of outdoor camping, in a best-of-both-worlds scenario. It's mainly for the romantic or those with romantic prospects. Just as you'd see on a luxury hotel balcony on the Riviera, glampers can be spotted sipping champagne by candlelight on decks with ocean views or expanses of green rolling hills dotted with bovine grass-eaters. Their glamp will be just as good if not better than an Airbnb—and the best thing is, it's always set up before they arrive. Glamping is particularly attractive to newlyweds, kid-free elders or those wanting to impress the underpants off their new lover. It often involves a spacious white- canvas bell tent with solid floor and minimal, no-fuss furniture – bar the bed, which is, more often than not, the main attraction. Think Bedouin, British Army Corps, or an explorer looking for a lost city. You can leave the burbs and go glamping without the need for camping gear, four-wheel-drive recovery kits or gumboots. You can wear your heels and best linen shirt while maintaining your expensive blow-wave, and have enough privacy to break out the lacy knickers.

Camping trailer

Camping trailers have come a long way since the days when Dad would convert the old box trailer into a magical mobile cubby house. They're more popular than electric scooters! Those with a thin wallet can get a brand newy for under $10,000, though the average cost is around $25–30,000. Those with buckets of folding can go up to $80,000, no probs. Camping trailers don't seem to hold their value, so if things are tight, go online and pick up a bewdy for just a few grand. But beware: there are some shockers out there, so the more you spend, the better the quality, onboard facilities and accessories. If you're towing off-road, you'll need a trailer built to withstand dust, potholes, corrugations and the wrath of Mother Nature.

A camper trailer will allow you to get into places that caravans can only dream of. Most trailer sailors like to get right out of the way and park by a river, beach or on a perch with a million-dollar view. Then they unhitch the bulletproof box and transform it into a fold-out glamping condo. It's all about going off-grid and being totally autonomous, with solar power, kitchen, a decent-sized water tank, outside shower – just like a van, but more outdoorsy.

Apart from dodgy homemade jobs, there are three varieties to choose from.

Soft-floor trailer

The soft-floor trailer is a lightweight, basic option that takes a bit more time and help to set up, but is easier on your towing vehicle. There's more floor space, but you then need to make up beds as well.

Hard-floor trailer

These bewdies have ready-made beds, pull-out kitchens and a sealed body to keep out dust and weather. They're quick and easy to set up, usually with the press of a button or pull of a lever. With large water capacity and a ute-load of extra options, these are great for a couple or a family, and for going off-grid.

Hybrid

As the name suggests, hybrid trailers are a cross between an off-road caravan and a trailer, giving you the best of both worlds. They usually come with all the features of a hard-floor but with added extras, such as hot water on tap and a gourmet kitchen, and they're built to withstand the rigours of long dirt roads with twin shockies and a hard exterior shell.

Before you decide which type of camper trailer is for you, tick off what's important to you from the list below, then take it from there:

- fridge and/or freezer
- awning
- hot-and-cold shower
- heating system
- onboard toilet facilities
- solar panels
- drop-down stabiliser legs
- LED lighting
- stove or electric cooker
- storage space
- pressurised wash taps

Popular free camp on the Mary River, Western Australia.

Caravan

These homes away from home are like cubby houses on wheels for grown-ups, but way more comfortable. If you're challenged by the outdoors, have sore bones, are averse to sleeping on the ground or you're a born cave-dweller, hook one up and it'll follow you wherever you choose to go.

But before you commit, ask yourself if you'll be going off-road or sticking to the blacktop; if you'll be going solo with your sweetheart or roving with the whole tribe (and what about Fido?); *and* how long you want to go away for. This'll help you work out what van suits your needs and the kinds of places you can stay.

You should also check the towing capacity of your vehicle and the fully laden weight of the van you want to tow.

Your budget will play a major part in your decision-making. New vans are pricey and second-hand ones might be half rattled to death.

Once you have thrashed all this out it's time to decide which one.

Entry level $

- Smaller, fixed layout, double bed, side dining area, small kitchen, minimal or no bathroom

- Easier to park and tow, gets into smaller out-of-the-way spaces

- Might need to be in a caravan park or bush location for ablutions

Family $$

- Bigger, sleeps 4–6, larger dining area, small bathroom
- Slightly bigger kitchen area
- Easier with kids
- Best suited for caravan parks with all the amenities

Luxury $$$

- Most comforts of home, including big double bedroom, spacious dining and kitchen, bathroom with chemical toilet, entertainment systems, bunks and/or 2–4 single beds

- Needs decent-sized vehicle/towing capacity – preferably 4WD to tow, less manoeuvrable

- With solar can be fully autonomous, allowing you to stay out of caravan parks

Mega $$$$

- The works: spacious everything, dishwasher, washing machine, large fridge, expandable, the list goes on

- Not suitable for every caravan park

- Needs plenty of grunt under the car bonnet

- Usually fully autonomous with solar power and large water capacity

THE ORIGINAL CAMPER TRAILER

If you thought your camper trailer was a little antiquated, take a trip to the Australian Motorlife Museum in Wollongong and step back 115 years to what must be the very first fully imported commercially built camper trailer in Australia, if not the world.

The Auto-Kamp trailer was manufactured in California in 1910 and shipped by steamer to Sydney, then on to Tasmania. After a rigorous life of camping throughout Tassie it was lovingly restored by Tasmanian Bill Weston, then shipped back to the mainland and loaned to the museum. It was designed to be towed by a Ford Model T via a hitch, which looked like something out of *The Flintstones*.

An accompanying brochure extols the virtues of this marvellous new invention, much of which still applies today.

> The instinct for a free life in the wide world out-of-doors is as natural and wholesome as the gratification of hunger and thirst and love. It is Nature's recall to the simple mode of existence that she intended for us. In every one of us there is a dash of gypsy that can bring up visions of green fields and far rolling hills, of tall forests and swift flowing streams. To be free, to go or come at one's own sweet will, to do this or that or nothing, to bask or sport in the clean out-doors.

The Auto-Kamp trailer doubles the possibilities of the automobile. For a day's outing or long tour, the Auto-Kamp gives you a completely equipped home, comfortable beds with sagless springs and mattresses, gasoline stove, ice box, electric light and other conveniences. There is plenty of room for everything, leaving full freedom of the car to its occupants. Everything is securely packed and entirely protected from dust, mud or rain.

There is the intense satisfaction of knowing that you can go exactly where you like, when you like and can stay as long as you like and the total expense will be very, very slight. You are quite likely to find it cheaper than staying at home.

The go-anywhere 4WD motorhome, Napier Range, Kimberley, Western Australia.

Campervan and mobile home

If you like pulling up wherever you can get to and staying over, these all-in-one combined drive, eat and sleep mobiles are your answer. They come in all shapes and sizes, with four-wheel drives, pop-tops, fold-out canopies, tiny kitchens and somewhere to sleep.

BARRY

Travelling solo with his modified van

Winton, outback Queensland

I met Barry while having a beer at the Australian Hotel in Winton. A quiet, well-travelled and gentle man, he has a cheerful and welcoming spirit.

'I'm originally from Dunedoo, but I spent twenty years in Melbourne and retired in 2018,' he told me. 'I did some house-sitting for a couple of years to see how I liked it and then decided I wanted to go caravanning.'

Barry bought himself a second-hand caravan. It took him more than six months to modify it. 'I cut the bed back and made that into a king single. I wanted a good mattress, so I paid quite a bit of money for that,' he told me. 'I cut the wardrobe back to make more room to get around the bed and cut a cupboard out. I then had room for a shower, a washbasin and a toilet. I installed a good-sized fridge that runs off solar, a range hood and a cooktop. The fridge is an EvaKool. It's a compressor fridge, and it doesn't run on gas or 240 volt. There's 100 litres of fridge and 40 litres of freezer storage. I didn't want an oven, because it just creates grease. I've got my microwave. I got the bench tops from Bunnings and cut them back.'

I asked him what kind of battery storage he had.

'Four hundred amp hours of lithium battery, and on the roof I've got 760 watts of solar.'

Barry preferred to free camp, with the occasional stay in caravan parks.

'Until I came into this caravan park two days ago, I'd been free camping probably for a fortnight or more. I'm just topping up my batteries now with the battery charger. I do a bit of farm-sitting, but at the moment I'm not taking on those jobs, because I want to see some countryside.'

'What's your idea of free camping?' I asked him.

'No power, no water, so you're going to have your own. You've got bigger areas, so you might not have anyone for 50 or 20 metres away.'

'Do you get lonely?'

'No. You meet so many interesting people. You go to the pub and talk to the locals and you find out all sorts of different things.'

At 76, Barry seemed to still be going strong. 'I'll keep going for another couple of years maybe – I don't know. But I won't get sick of it, that's for sure.'

All sorted then

So after endless nights of pillow talk you've nutted out your dream destination, how you're going to get there and whether it's a long weekend backpacking or a month in a canvas condominium. Now might be the time to check the piggy bank to make sure you've got enough coin to fork out for some things that will make sure you get back alive, enlightened and still able to afford to feed the kids. Because there are a few more things to think about before you head out the driveway, as you'll find out in Chapter 4.

Thomas Jungala Rice with his freshly painted Ngappa car, Yuendumu, Northern Territory.

THE RAINMAKING MISSION

Yuendumu to Broome via The Tanami Track – September 2001

The last episode of *Bush Mechanics* required a trip along the Tanami Track from Yuendumu to Broome. The idea was to do a modern-day re-enactment of an ancient custom and trade route that saw pearl shell being traded from the Broome area all the way down to desert groups like those that now live at Yuendumu. The shells were used in various ceremonial capacities, such as the fire ceremony Jardiwanpa, but more commonly for making rain.

It was decided we needed a large car with plenty of room inside for filming and enough comfort to carry our five bush mechanic stars; Simeon, Errol, Boobadoo (Steven), Junior and Randle all the way to Broome. A Ford Fairlane would do the job nicely.

I sourced one via a trade magazine in Adelaide and had it freighted up to Alice Springs. It was then driven out to Yuendumu to get ready for the big drive. Because it was going to be used on a cultural mission to get pearl shell, Francis was keen to sing it (embody it within the realm of its given Dreaming story) and get it painted in the correct Kurruwarri (traditional design) for the Ngappa Jukurrpa, or rain Dreaming.

We approached Thomas Jungala Rice, who is royalty when it comes to traditional Warlpiri knowledge and law. He was happy to paint the car and sing it, plus he was the correct man according to kinship and Warlpiri ownership, and he was a custodian of the Ngappa songline. He picked a secret out-of-the-way spot to get on with the job. We visited him a few times to check on his progress. He had a smoky fire going by the car and was lightly singing the Ngappa Jukurrpa under his breath as he adorned the Ford with acrylic paint. He used slow brushstrokes with the same Kurruwarri that appear in paintings, on bodies, in cave art and on ground paintings. The design is part of a complex rain-Dreaming songline that traverses a large portion of Warlpiri Country and involves the creation of clouds, serpents, lightning and a place called Juka Juka, a striking collection of large granite rocks that point up into the sky that were left behind by the kurdukurdu mangkurdu (children of the rain Dreaming, or young clouds) who camped there one night.

Jungala got word to us that the Ford was ready, that we should come and pick it up, and that Francis was to bring boomerangs. When we arrived, Jungala proudly showed off his artwork, then proceeded to sing it with boomerang-clapping accompaniment.

KURRUWARRI

Kurruwarri are traditional Aboriginal designs and patterns that relate to a particular songline or Dreaming narrative. They form the basis of paintings on canvas, bodies and ground paintings, and represent animals, people and places that are central to the Dreaming story.

JUKURRPA

Jukurrpa is a western-desert Aboriginal word that is now broadly used by most Aboriginal groups and the art world, and which translates as 'songlines', 'Dreaming' or 'the Dreamtime'. This conceptual Dreamtime often includes creation stories, kinship and land features. It's manifested in paintings, ceremonies and song cycles. Jukurrpa is often the basis of a code of conduct and moral and spiritual laws that govern Aboriginal society.

Being a law man as well, Francis joined in, and they both sang the ancient and magical high pitch then low grumbly tones at the car in full-throttled harmony as only the Warlpiri can do.

From that moment the Ford Fairlane became known as 'the Ngappa Car', or the rain-Dreaming car.

We drove the car back to Yuendumu. Along the way people waved and stared wide-eyed, grinning and yelling 'Ngappa Car! Ngutju nyiani! [Good one!]' We were almost ready to hit the Tanami Track, and had loaded the support Toyota with camera gear, swags and tucker for the long and arduous journey to Broome.

The boys seemed to be in an unsettled mood and not their usual exuberant selves. Then Simeon wandered up and expressed some concerns about going to Broome.

'Broome's rubbish place, Jupurrurla. They got cheeky police there. They lock you up for nothing.'

Then Errol Nelson chipped in.

'Yeah, they locked up Murray for three months just 'cause he was from the NT!'

Then Simeon came out with a truth that nearly knocked me over.

'The other thing is, Jupurrurla ... We got no paper.'

In my naivety I had assumed the boys had their licences all along. Now I'd had a Warlpiri reality check.

'So the whole time we've been filming, the past few weeks, none of you had a licence?'

Simeon and Errol shuffled about.

'Nothing ... cops took it.'

To be driving around the bush tracks, local roads and a few trips into Alice and back without a licence was one thing, but to drive all the way through several Kimberley towns to Broome in a beat-up old car painted up with a traditional rain-Dreaming design was something else.

'Well, we need someone with a licence,' I said. 'Know anyone?' I asked, as if it was as improbable as finding Lasseter's lost gold.

After some contemplation and fast Warlpiri chatter that went beyond my kindergarten-level understanding of the ancient language, they had a solution – or, more to the point, a victim.

'Davey!' Simeon announced with glee. 'He's got that paper.'

'Yeah! He's half Warlpiri, half Arrernte, but still a good bloke,' Errol announced excitedly. 'He lives at Amoonguna in town and doesn't drink, but he's a Tjapaltjarri.'

All the boys including myself were Jupurrurlas, which made us brothers in the kinship system. We had equal and level standing with each other. Tjapaltjarris were outside our moiety, but according to the Warlpiri kinship system, this made Tjapaltjarris our brothers-in-law, who are obliged to do whatever we ask.

SKIN NAMES

Skin names exist throughout Aboriginal Australia in different forms. They are a means of determining a person's place within a kinship system. In some areas, particularly in central Australia among the Warlpiri, Luritja and Pintubi, they are strongly adhered to, with most people referred to by their skin name only.

This skin name will determine a person's role, responsibilities and obligations to others, to ceremonial business and to the land.

This system of social organisation differs among the various tribal and language groups. Some language groups, like the Pitjantjatjara, rarely use skin names at all.

So if Davey was in Yuendumu, he had no choice but to come with us as driver. We loaded the last few things and drove to Davey's mother's house, where he was staying with his wife and kids. Unannounced, the Ngappa car and Toyota pulled up out the front and Davey emerged from the house.

'Tjapaltjarri! You got that paper?' Simeon yelled out from the rear passenger seat.

'Yuwai,' Davey responded cautiously in the affirmative.

'You're the driver now,' Simeon declared.

'Where we going?'

'Broome.'

Culturally obliged to follow orders from five Jupurrurlas (including me), Davey got behind the wheel without another word, and we were off.

The Ngappa car, painted up with the ancient symbols and patterns or Kurruwarri of the rain Dreaming, would be driving through the very country the Ngappa songline cuts through. Not only that, in the belly of the motorised Dreaming car were four men who were Jupurrurlas, skin brothers with the correct custodial relationship to the Ngappa Dreaming, going all the way to Broome on a mission from the ancestors to bring on some much-needed rain!

A few million corrugations up the track, we called into Rabbit Flat Roadhouse for fuel. While there, different cars with Warlpiri occupants pulled up. The Ngappa car produced a universal reaction, as it was no longer just a car: it had transmogrified into a mobile representative of the Ngappa Jukurrpa. Its painted icons were immediately recognised by all Warlpiri people. They would walk over and caress the car as if it was the living embodiment of a narrative they all knew and were comforted by. For some, it would invoke the ancient Ngappa Jukurrpa song cycle, which they would sing under their breath while touching the car's newly acquired artwork.

Happy in its new role as cultural ambassador, the Ngappa car was performing nicely and the filming going just as nicely. It was pretty hard not to get inspired while behind the camera in dramatic country with a classic car painted in the correct traditional design retracing an ancient trade route. What could go wrong?

An automatic gearbox is a thing of mystery and wonder. Somehow an oily fluid navigates its way through a maze of cast alloy and affects another metal box full of planet gears, sun gears, ring gears, bands and valves, then engages first, right up to third or fourth gear, and even reverse. On the second day of filming on the long, dusty and corrugated Tanami Track, the magic that connected the mighty V8 motor to the gearbox disappeared. Even though we had a car full of expert bush mechanics, no amount of hitting, oil checking or spraying with tinned lubricant could get the transmission to engage with the motor. We still had a few days of driving to get to Halls Creek in the Kimberley and we were too far to turn back. Plus we had a TV show to make! Our predicament was not part of the plan.

I dragged out my trusty Flying Doctor radio from behind the back seat, alligator-clipped it to the battery and threw the antenna wire over a mulga tree. I rang Jen, the *Bush Mechanics* producer, who was still back in Yuendumu.

'We're halfway up the Tanami and the gearbox has had it. Over.'

'Oh no! What can I do? Over.'

'See if there's one at the Alice Springs wreckers, I'll call back in a few hours. Over and out.'

While Jen was looking for a second-hand gearbox, we had to work out how we could keep filming with a car that had gone on strike. This was done via a few very dodgy methods:

1. Towing the Ngappa car and filming from a distance while framing out the tow car and rope.

2. Shunting the car from behind with the bull bar of our support vehicle, then applying the brakes and filming it rolling till it stopped.

3. Filming from the back of the car towing the Ngappa car.

I got back to Jen – she'd found the right gearbox in Alice. She'd pick it up and drive it to Yuendumu, where an air-charter company would collect it and take it to Halls Creek. We'd be there in two days to collect it from the airport.

We continued filming. Towing a car on a rocky dirt road is like having a crowd of angry protesters throwing rocks at their worst enemy.

Jen McMahon and Peter Bartlett load a replacement gearbox into a
Cessna, Yuendumu, Northern Territory.

By the time we reached the outskirts of Hells Crack – correction,
Halls Creek – rocks from the towing car had smashed the
Ngappa car's windscreen, the headlights and the front blinkers,
and had chipped off a few layers of paint.

Luckily, the Halls Creek main street is on a hill, so we could
unleash the tow vehicle and make out that the boys had run out
of petrol, then roll into the servo to fill up.

We picked up the gearbox from the airstrip and went on the
hunt for a mechanic with a hoist to do the job. They all declined
to even look at it! After pleading with an Aboriginal-owned
resource centre, we were allowed access to their mechanical
workshop and hoist, but only between the hours of 6 pm and
6 am. My camera assistant Hughey, who is now in high demand
as a highly talented cinematographer, was also a fully qualified
mechanic.

It was also handy that Davey, our new driver, was strong as a rogue bull – lifting the gearbox and bell housing was not for featherweights.

Hughey, Davey and I worked under the Ngappa car all through the night, and by dawn we had the new gearbox in and filled with magic fluid. It was running and going through the gears like a Ferrari … well, that's what it seemed like to us.

Blurry eyed and semi-conscious, Davey picked up the boys from various locations around town in the Ngappa car and we left bad ol' Hells Crack en route to Broome. My next mission was to find a windscreen so the boys would attract less attention from the evil cops in Broome. They'd also be able to drive in relative comfort rather than sitting in a perpetual cyclone wearing cheap servo sunnies.

I rang my son Chris, who was living in Broome, and asked him to look for a suitable windscreen at the Broome wreckers and meet us at Fitzroy Crossing a few hundred kilometres up the road. On the drive we encountered bushfires, rain and people cheering us on.

We met Chris, who fortunately had found the correct windscreen. But to keep any kind of story integrity for the show we couldn't just suddenly have a windscreen appear on the Ngappa car. So, I had the boys stop for a piss in the bush on the outskirts of Fitzroy Crossing and point. 'Oh, look, there's a windscreen that just happens to be the right one for a 1973 Ford Fairlane!' Don't believe everything you see on TV!

Windscreen glued on, we were back on the road to Broome. When we finally got there, we went straight to Cable Beach to meet Bardi man Stephen Albert, also known as Baamba, who had the pearl shells the boys were there to collect.

Baamba was sitting in a makeshift humpy near the sand dunes. The boys emerged from the Ngappa car, greeted Baamba and ceremoniously received the pearl shells. Mission accomplished – so far.

With shells in hand, the boys returned home to Yuendumu and passed them on to the rainmaking boss: old Jungala Rice, the man who painted the car. In no time, he went out to a dry claypan and sang the rainmaking songline while holding the shells up to the sky. It immediately started spitting with rain. The following day, big dark clouds formed, accompanied by endless displays of lightning.

It rained for days. The immediate area and country to the west experienced floods never seen in living memory. The small Pintubi community of Kiwirrkurra in Western Australia went under water and the place was evacuated. It was 18 months before residents could return home.

The Ngappa car sat at my house in Broome for over a year, gaining notoriety while the acrylic-paint adornment cracked and crazed under the intense heat, humidity and rain of a Broome wet season. Eventually, a visionary from the Melbourne Museum acquired it for their collection. It was trucked down and sat in relative obscurity for a few more years. Then the National Motor Museum added it to their travelling *Bush Mechanics* exhibition.

The Batty gang with the Ngappa car, Broome, Western Australia.

But the power of the Ngappa Jukurrpa 1973 Ford Fairlane ZF didn't stop there. A few years ago, I was commissioned to create a replica of the same car with the same Ngappa Kurruwarri painted on it for the Australian Centre of the Moving Image (ACMI) in the heart of Melbourne's CBD, next to Federation Square.

The Ngappa car is not only a relic from a popular TV show, it's a vehicle that carries a deep connection to Country, the ancient songlines that traverse it and the unique place of the Warlpiri in a changing modern world.

Me with the Ngappa car replica at ACMI (Australian Centre for Moving Image) Federation Square, Melbourne, Victoria.

 Watch Video: Painting the Songlines

4

Family camp on the road to Broome.

BUSH-BASHING ESSENTIALS

The trip I took to Alice with my five-year-old son back in 1981 was the beginning of a whole new life and a whole new family. We stayed, and before long I had not one but four kids. Each year we'd load up whatever vehicle I had created in the backyard and hit the road to spend Christmas in Wollongong. Then, after 12 years in Alice, we moved to Broome, a few thousand kilometres north west, and the annual Wollongong trip became two weeks each way. With all kids on board we'd traverse the country with everything we needed packed neatly on the roof or in the ute or the tub of a twin cab. We had no caravan, and no trailer!

I took pride in being fully self-reliant, so we could stop and make camp each night along the way, only staying in motels if there was no other option. Our deadline was Christmas Eve, so we could usually find time to stop for a while once we hit a beach on the east coast.

Family camp, Mary River, Western Australia.

We all totally loved these drives. We'd often take different routes: along the Murray, through the Hay Plains, down the Tanami Track, the Stuart Highway, the Plenty – you name it, we drove it. The most important thing was the ability to find a place to camp along the way, which usually meant swagging under the stars or, if required, in the ol' centre-pole tent. I'd prep and cook the evening meal on the tailgate while Mum and the kids would unroll the swags and collect firewood.

Our Christmas trips down south have become the stuff of family lore. They have instilled a sense of adventure in my now grown-up kids and given them all a solid grounding in what's required for a long road trip. I still travel this way, and it remains one of my all-time favourite things to do. And after stints in the big smoke, my kids have returned to the places they call home – Alice Springs and Broome – so it's as good an excuse as any to hit the road each winter and go north.

But like most things, it's all in the preparation.

Be prepared!

The act of 'going bush' can be a simple, quiet weekend camp or a full-on, bone-through-the-nose, once-in-a-lifetime near-death adventure, and degrees in between. There are any number of outdoor thrillseeker shops to kit up at, depending on how, when and where you might want to go and the gear you'll need once you get there. For bushwalkers, canoeists, picnickers or daytrippers, there are mountains of specialist gizmos, featherweight tents, self-inflating mattresses – the list goes on.

Apart from the obvious, such as something to sleep in, a basic tool kit, a spare key, a cooker and a first-aid kit, there are a few essential items that I reckon make long-distance travelling a breeze: a billy box, a tuckerbox, an esky or car fridge, and an in-built water tank with a tap on the back of the vehicle. You'll learn about all of these things and more in this section of the book so that you're not caught off guard when you're out bush.

Camping with my daughter Gina by the Murrumbidgee River near Hay, New South Wales.

Spare tyre

Not carrying a spare tyre is akin to not wearing gum boots in a cowshed ... without one you're in deep shit. You might think car manufacturers are required to provide one with every new car by law, but this is not the case. Many smaller cars only come with emergency wheels known as donuts, which restrict you to 80km/h or a puncture-repair kit and can of sealant. If you are going beyond the outskirts of the village, make sure you've got a spare tyre, that it's inflated and that you know how to change it. If you're going remote, always carry a second spare. If you're going really remote, take a second spare, a tyre-plugging kit and a compressor (more on those later). There are unsealed roads out there that shred tyres, no matter how new, how expensive or how hyped-up those tyres might be. I've learnt the hard way and limped into a town or community with my last unpunctured tyre exhaling its final gasp.

In an absolutely desperately deflated situation, where your life depends on it, or if you're just bone-lazy and willing to do untold additional damage to your wagon, you can just keep driving with the flat till the rubber gives up and you're down on the rim. This is a common occurrence in more remote parts of our vast land. Not advised!

After some hard yards, Tanami track, Northern Territory.

Then there are the good ol', bad ol' split rims: a wheel assembly consisting of multiple pieces joined together by bolts or a lock ring. These have been around about as long as 4WD cars went bush. Some purist diehards swear by them, others are glad the tubeless came along. They can have up to a ten-ply rating and require a tube. I've seen split rims easily changed in the bush by levering off the retaining ring with tyre irons, patching the puncture and putting it back together again. But if you get the procedure wrong you can take your face off with a flying retaining ring. They do deliver the genuine old school look.

Repairing a puncture on a split rim, Great Sandy Desert, Western Australia.

Car jack

Consumer laws ensure that every vehicle sold in Australia comes with a jack, which is super handy for lifting the car to change a flat tyre. Jacks vary in type and weight capability: there are screw jacks, scissor jacks, lever jacks, bottle jacks and a variety of others. Everybody who gets behind the wheel of a car should know where the jack is located and how to use it.

The idea is to use the jack to raise the vehicle, preferably by putting the jack under the axle or a point below the wheel (or wheels) in trouble. Lifting the body of the car is the wrong way to go. It means raising the jack much higher, making it more dangerous and potentially running out of lift.

For the bush basher, a second jack is a must. I always carry a medium-sized hydraulic bottle jack.

If you're going off-road a lot, chances are you'll get bogged or get a puncture at some stage. This can cause your car to sit low on the ground, making it difficult to get to a jack point underneath. A bottle jack will allow you to lift the car from a more accessible point, so you can get your supplied jack under the axle.

In a totally disastrous situation, an inflatable bag jack can lift you out of car-consuming mud or quicksand, or a kanga jack will lift the side of your car a metre in the air. Both the bag jack and especially the kanga jack are about as safe as a one-wheel rollerskate. Use at your peril!

But my all-time favourite, multi-purpose, organic and vegan-friendly jack is a length of mulga on an anthill. This is the means of lifting a car favoured by bush mechanics and bushies Australia wide. With the help of a bit of muscle you can even lift it high enough to place a prop under the car and remove any number of things, including the tail shaft, gearbox and even the differential.

A wheel brace

A wheel brace is an essential item for removing wheel nuts, which is particularly handy when you need to change a tyre. Don't be fooled by the dinky bent hunk of steel with a socket welded on the end that the car manufacturers might try to pass off as a tool for doing the same job. They save billions each year by skimping on this item. They may claim it's a multi-purpose tool with a chiselled end in case you want to open a can of paint, but these implements are annoying and cumbersome. Get yourself a good ol' wheel brace: it's a metal cross with four different wheel-nut sizes. It's easy to use and gives you good leverage on the nuts.

Jumper leads

A great way to make yourself super popular at the viewing-area car park or the remote camping ground is to be the happy camper with the jumper leads when a distressed driver comes asking for help. The number of times I've brought a dead car back to life for a total stranger! But you're just as likely to need the spark of life to revive your own lifeless chariot. Fork out that little bit extra and get a good set that matches your vehicle, or just get the heavy-duty ones straight up, especially if you are running a diesel or have a big donk under the hood. Look for quality copper clamps with a strong grip, and get them at least 3 metres long. Keep the donor car running – you may have to allow a few minutes once connected to get a bit of charge into the dead battery.

Air compressor

 If you travel in a four-wheel drive and venture beyond school pick-ups and the shopping-centre car park, an air compressor is as essential as a chocolate bar on a long drive. Basically, an air compressor is a scaled-down version of the machine you use at the service station to check the air pressure in your tyres. They come with a built-in pressure gauge, which is super handy when lowering your tyre pressure to match the road surface or terrain. (Less air in your tyres makes some off-roading much more pleasant – until of course there is *no* air in your tyres and you wind up stranded.)

Sand can be an unpredictable bogging trap. It can look solid, but a few millimetres under that sunbaked crust might lie a bottomless pit of despair. If you're going anywhere near the stuff, you need to have a decent air compressor. With an explosion in sales of self-contained, go-anywhere van and trailer rigs, coastal and river camps are more often than not the preferred destination. For Cape Leveque, Ningaloo, Finke River and a truckload of other dream destinations, having one is an absolute must—unless you're hoping to camp in sand for a few days till you're rescued.

Some adventurers tend to spark it up at the thought of a bit of dirt, while others wait till the corrugations have rattled their bones, passengers and the contents of their van into submission before they'll let the tyres down. If they resist, or don't carry one on board, they may well end up churning away in sand in low range, moving 2 miles an hour, or sink to the floor with the wheels spinning, mocking their stupidity.

This raises the age-old question of how far you should let the tyre pressure down. A simple rule of thumb is to read the conditions and do the minimal air exit first up, then if the sand or gravel is too soft and deep, let out more. The first let down can be to about 170 kPa (25 psi), then if need be, to 140 kPa (20 psi), then if the going is really tough, down to 100 kPa (15 psi). Any less than this might wreck your tyres and lower your ground clearance, which can create its own problems and require a winch, flares or an unscheduled camp in sand.

When selecting the air compressor, spend as much as you can. As a rubbish-dump gleaner, I've seen hundreds of the cheap ones given the chuck. After one compression session the cylinder overheats and melts to a blob of molten metal. A decent one has a long hose and a long battery or lighter lead, as well as a built-in pressure gauge.

Hyundai pulls Suzuki out of mud hole, Ramingining, Arnhem Land, Northern Territory.

Snatch strap

A snatch strap is not a nocturnal mutual-gratification device, but a modern-day tow rope. I've seen every kind of towing medium known to motoring. The *Bush Mechanics* and *Black As* boys were particularly fond of cutting out the seatbelts and tying them together, making a short and spectacularly dangerous tow. Clothes, particularly denim jeans, work okay if you want to drive on in your undies. Then there's the solid length of mulga tied on with fencing wire, which is actually pretty effective. But gone are the days when your only option to tow another car or pull a desperately bogged bush basher out of quicksand was a length of fencing wire.

Snatch straps come in varying lengths and breaking strains, have loops at both ends and roll up like a fire hose. They possess a certain amount of spring like a giant rubberband, so when the puller pulls it, the pulled springs out of the bog and back to solid ground.

FENCING WIRE

Fencing wire comes in a variety of thicknesses, tensile strengths and degrees of softness. As well as being deployed to make fences to contain animals, fencing wire is used to tie together two or more lengths of timber to metal in a myriad of applications, the common one being corrugated iron in the construction of sheds, chook pens, humpies and lean to's. Soft fencing wire is the most useful and durable. Back in the day, stockyards, huts and any number of wooden frames or structures were held together with fencing wire. To use it effectively, all that's required is a pair of pliers and the Queensland hitch, otherwise known as the Cobb & Co hitch.

MULGA WOOD

Mulga is a type of acacia tree that populates vast areas of Australia's inland. It's slow growing, drought resistant and one of the hardest timbers around. For desert tribes, it's the go-to timber for boomerangs, clap sticks and digging or fighting sticks called nulla nullas.

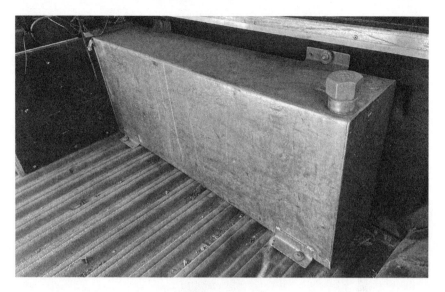

Water tank

You can have the flashest four-wheel drive, the latest blow-up tent and roof racks laden with pushbikes and fishing gear – but you won't go far without the old H_2O. You'll need to take heaps of the stuff. If you're overnight bushwalking and having to carry water, the rule of thumb is to allow 4 litres per person per day.

Back in the day, preparing for a long road trip meant foraging around the shed for camping and long-distance-travelling gear, then coming out with a 10- or 20-litre container for water and throwing that in back of the ute. On the road, as metres turned into kilometres and kilometres into days, getting to the water container buried under beach towels, tents, tool bags and on-road essentials became harder than finding a dollar coin for a shopping trolley. Then there's the leaking container that soaks everything that's anywhere near it.

After buying an old HiLux with a built-in stainless-steel water tank with a tap in the tray on the back, I've never looked at a plastic vessel again. Since this aquamonious discovery I have always had one in my long-distance vehicles. A 100-litre tank will usually last five to seven days on the road if you're using it for drinking, cooking and the occasional face wash or billy bath. It was a lifesaver when we had babies or small children on board, helping to maintain a harmonious cabin ambience without the permeating pong of the brown trouser deposit. We would simply pull up and wash the offending rear end under the tap on the back.

Carrying good drinking water is a particularly good idea to ensure you're not relying on local tap water, which can be salty bore water, full of particles like uranium or taste like the overflow of a septic tank.

Swag

Proceed with caution, as I'm about to bag the modern swag!

Swags entered the Australian lexicon via our tear-jerking alternative national anthem, 'Waltzing Matilda'. What most people don't know is that the song is inspired by a true story. Back in the

1890s, unionised shearers went on strike and walked off the sheep stations, carrying their swags with them. The shearers had got pretty worked up about non-union labour working for peanuts, and went on a rampage, burning shearing sheds and killing sheep. They became known as swagmen. One of the swagmen camped by a billabong near Winton in western Queensland. Army troopers were eventually sent in to settle the score, but poor old shearer and swagman Sam Hoffmeister took his own life before the troopers could cart him off to jail.

So today we celebrate a shearer with a swag who martyred himself for the glory of the union movement. The swag is therefore sacrosanct, enshrined in Australian folklore. A swag brings comfort, company and a good night's rest under the stars. It invokes our inner swagman or swagwoman and gives rise to the spirited nature lover in us all. We rise with the sun invigorated, refreshed and ready to bathe in the nearest billabong.

In recent years, tent-like creations have surfaced in the image of our sacred swag. But they are not swags – to call a tent a swag is an act of blasphemy. A *real* swag is a simple strip of foam rubber wrapped in heavy-duty canvas, with a zip down one or both sides and roomy enough for a doona, pillow and sheets. A *real* swag has a flap that you can pull over your head to fend off moisture from the heavens. A *real* swag is grounded by nature and provides a comfy resting place by the fire, where swagmen and swagwomen can doze, chat or enjoy combined horizontal pleasure-seeking on a firm surface. Small canvas tents are fine – but they are not swags.

Chair

Some things are just *not* for sitting on – like the esky, which is a total no-no when it comes to seating arrangements. It's the duty of all camp captains to inform fellow campers of this rule, to maintain harmony and ready access to cold beer. Sitting on the ground is okay when there's no other option, but being elevated is more civilised and saves your travel-weary body the effort of repeatedly getting up off the ground then down again.

A pet hate of mine is the collapsible chair that populates camping stores and camping grounds throughout the country, its influence spreading faster than crotch rash. They come with all kinds of add-ons, such as stubby holders, neck rests and leg rests, but they all result in the same thing: sagging discomfort and terminal deterioration. Just go to a camping ground skip bin after Christmas and see the piles of ripped canvas and broken bones of the doomed collapsibles. They've not only collapsed, but completely fallen apart (and have probably caused near-fatal injuries to the previously happy camper).

It's not just the two-dollar-shop variety – it's all of them, even the doubles. Director's chairs are not much better and seem to be particularly sensitive to Earth's gravitational pull, resulting in the sitter falling backwards and wearing their freshly made champagne cocktail to the waiting room of the nearest emergency department (which might be half a day away).

What's wrong with a good ol' heavy-duty steel-and-plastic fold-up chair? I've sat in them elevated above mud, snow, sand and rock. I've also had countless interviewees sit firmly and at a nice height and eyeline for my camera. I wouldn't dare ask an older person to sit in one of the sag bags for an in-depth interview in case they are never able to get up again. I've carted my small collection of fold-up chairs to all corners of the country and sat comfortably and safely for decades. Get them at your local hardware store. The only downside is working out how to pack them, but I find the roof rack and a few tie-down straps do the job.

Another, more compact sitting device is the good old folding canvas chair. The ones with a fold-out back strap are gold. They pack away easily, they're light and they last a lifetime.

Light

Most people will have a torch feature on their mobile phone. This is fine for the few seconds you need to find the real torch, but otherwise save the battery on your mobile for checking likes on your Facebook posts, if you're still in range. There are other ways to see in the dark!

Forget relying on candles, firesticks, matches or lighters to illuminate your way to the wee tree. Instead, launch yourself into the modern world of LED. Otherwise known as light-emitting diodes, this fabulous little invention has been around since valve radios. When I was a kid, my father and I made a crystal set radio with a diode as the main component. There was no battery, no power – the diode just magically picked up radio you could listen to with an earpiece.

LEDs use ten times less power than an old-school incandescent light with a bulb, and are bright as! This means you use fewer batteries, you don't drain your car battery and it's generally much better for our planet.

I like to have at least three LED lights when travelling or going bush: a head torch, a camping light and a good ol' handheld torch. The handheld speaks for itself, and it's best practice to return it to the same spot each time. The head torch is hands-free, featherweight and automatically shines whichever way you're looking. All you need is a head to mount it. A cheapo one is fine – who needs the six brightness settings and various flashing colours? Two settings – bright and less bright – is as handy as you'll need. The most important thing is to turn it off when you're talking to someone. Disregard this and you run the risk of being banned from the fire circle for life.

The camping light is usually a stationary item used to illuminate the cooking or food-prep area and give a general light to help prevent you going arse-up on a tent rope while looking for the billy for the next cuppa. They come in all shapes and sizes. Some have leads and plug into the cigarette lighter, while others have batteries. Since my chariot has a solar panel and independent battery, I find the cigarette lighter version suits me fine.

Billy box

If you're not bolted onto a caravan or trailer and prefer, like I do, to be unattached, this is for you. The billy box is the indestructible carry-all that houses an assortment of tea billies, camp ovens, cutlery, plates, cups, washing-up gear – in other words, everything you need to cook, eat with, drink from, boil water in and clean up.

The Batty Bush Bashing Billy Box (aka the BBBBB) is something other campers look at in awe. It has three separate sections and a built-in cutlery compartment, and I never go bush without it. Forty years old and still going strong, it sits fully packed and ready for action in a handy spot in the shed, and is corrugation proof, drop proof and (almost) dust proof. Constructed from 12-millimetre ply with a simple design, with handles on the side and a hinged lid, it's dead-easy to make. I've made several as presents, and a deluxe version out of marine ply for a wedding present.

Tuckerbox

The tuckerbox has the same dimensions as the billy box (which is handy for packing) and looks identical from the outside. But it has only one divider to separate tall bottles and containers from a shallow compartment for smaller things like herbs, stock cubes and spreads. It's for dry goods, cans and containers only. In the separate section I have a bottle of oil, bottle of wine, soy sauce, vinegar and other condiments.

Both the tuckerbox and billy box fit nicely in the tray of a ute, back of a wagon or boot of most cars. (Motorbikes, forget it.) They are virtually indestructible unless run over by a truck, which is exactly what happened to a tuckerbox of one of my sons.

BUSH COOKING 101

Everything tastes better in the bush. Maybe it's the fresh air, the near-starvation of a long hike, or your taste buds celebrating a break from the caviar and pheasant-liver pâté. The trick is to keep it  simple. (If you want some cooking ideas, at the back of this book you'll find a few of my favourite bush recipes.)

Non-perishable items

Stock up on a variety of your favourite tinned and packet food to save space in the esky or car fridge for chocolate biscuits and beer. Long-lasting food is also a great idea in case you get stuck in a flood, are bogged for a few days, break the motor or become stranded. This can happen to anyone on the wide-open road – including me more than a few times. And always remember to replenish supplies when you hit town. If your car fridge runs out of battery power or you can't refill your esky with fresh ice, there are some things that will go a few days or longer without being on ice, so long as they're kept out of the sun in a cool spot:

- zucchinis (they'll keep for a few days if fresh)
- pumpkins (uncut, they'll keep for weeks)
- long-life milk of all varieties, including powdered
- cooked meat
- bacon and preserved meats like salami
- smoked fish
- melons, citrus and most fresh fruits
- potatoes, sweet potatoes, onions and garlic
- dried fruit

Esky or car fridge

An esky with ice or a car fridge is a must for meat, veggies and dairy. If you can get block ice it will last way longer than crushed, but it's hard to find these days.

For decades I swore off car fridges. That's as a result of having to jump start too many cars in the morning after the fridge had sucked the life out of the battery overnight. I resisted calls from fellow travellers and film crews to invest a considerable amount of Johnny Cash just to keep a few things cool.

The downside to using an esky instead was the unpredictable availability of ice, which sometimes meant everything turned into a giant slushy with water leaking out, spoiling my dinner suit.

So, before my most recent drive to Broome (an annual event) I decided to get a car fridge. I went deep into the 'net, followed branches on Gumtree and scoured virtual marketplaces, only to decide to buy a brand newy! But which one? There are so many models and brands and sizes now. Back in the day, there only seemed to be one – the indestructible battery killer the Engel. But now everyone has one. It seems like every town in China has a car-fridge factory and an air freighter waiting at the airport ready to parachute them straight Down Under and into the utes and vans of every Aussie who's having a passing thought about going bush.

Online product reviews are a marvellous thing. They never lie. Why would they, unless there are teams of unscrupulous paid reviewers spending their days employed by multinationals to dream up glowing adjectives to sway the gullible fridge buyer? I have far more faith in humanity and internet integrity. The big brand names have got more stars than the Milky Way, but I have humble means and wanted something low-cost with at least 90 per cent

5-star reviews. I punched at the keys, waded through the whingers and weeded out the too-good-to-be-trues before settling on one.

It has already done a lap of Oz (including being tossed over corrugations so deep you could get lost in them) and it's come up trumps. It's a little bewdy and, most importantly, delivers an icy-cold beer every time I roll out the swag and get creative with my tuckerbox on the tailgate.

The mighty camp oven

If you're going to be cooking on a fire, you can't go past a camp oven. And once you've eaten from one, you'll be hooked for life. Camp ovens are easy to use, and they always deliver.

Even if the pack on your new camp oven says it's pre-seasoned, I recommend seasoning it anyway. This gives it a coating that prevents rust and a metal taste, helps hold flavours and makes it easier to clean.

To season your camp oven, scrub the inside of both pot and lid with dishwashing liquid, then rinse thoroughly and dry. Smear the inside with a little oil and then heat on a fire, barbecue or stove until it is smoking. Repeat once again.

You'll find some tasty camp-oven recipes in the back of this book.

 Watch Video: Kimberley Camp Cook

Ear candy

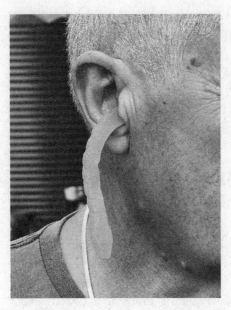

Now you have the wheels organised, toys packed, a destination in mind and a full tank of volts or dinosaur juice, you can head out your driveway and onto the open road, then sit back and enjoy the ride – ahhh. But when the kilometres turn into hundreds and thousands, a little audio enhancement will help the kilometres fly by. Music will fill the void for a while and, combined with your morning coffee hit, might even get you doing dance-floor moves behind the wheel.

But when the doof settles down to country favourites, it's time for some engrossing brain food. Just remember to download whatever you want to listen to before you head out into the high country. Here are a few options to get you started:

- **Radio** – If you're in range, radio is good for news and keeping up with the latest disasters.
- **Podcasts** – A great option, whether one-offs or serialised; pick from the humorous, dark or informative, depending on your taste.
- **Audiobooks** – A narrated book is perfect for a long drive. Just make sure everyone else in the car is on the same page and you not only like but can understand the reader.

Sartorial essentials

Hat

If you haven't yet convinced the grey matter and its surrounds that it needs to be kept in the shade, book your spot in the melanoma clinic while you still can. But note that American baseball, trucker and hip-hop caps are an insult to headwear.

Hats not only reduce upper-body toasting, but can instantly transform you into a cool-looking dude and make you look taller. I'm talking a broad round hat that shades not only your head and face but your neck, shoulders and ears as well. So long as it fits and casts a cancer-preventing shadow, you're way ahead of the burnt, hatless crowd.

My preference and all-time favourite is the palm-leaf hat. The palmy is lightweight and broad. If it gets crushed, it springs back into shape with a spray of water. In terms of style, it out-catwalks anything made from rabbit fur, canvas, straw or the gravity-burdened leather.

The palmy can be hard to find in cities, but once you're out bush, every outfitter, rodeo or station-supplies mob has racks of them. Wear it proud like an outback crown of glory, knowing you're in the company of genuine cowboys, bush legends, and style kings and queens of the bush.

Made in the shade

It takes little convincing that in bright sunny places like Australia, sunglasses are an absolute must. They help you look fabulous while covering your crow's-feet. Like hats, they also have health benefits, such as:

- protecting you from nasty UV rays
- helping to prevent skin cancers
- reducing eye strain and eye injuries
- preventing headaches

When it comes to choosing sunnies, don't skimp on the folding. So after you've decided on the style, brand and tint, I'd recommend you fork out a bit more for polarisation. Having an expensive brand name and a super trendy set of gogs perched on your nose is one thing, but if you're driving a car any distance or you're a keen fisher, polarisation is the way to look at the world. These tricky optical accessories have a built-in filter that blocks reflective glare and gives you the ability to see more clearly through windscreens and water.

I like to have two sets: a no-nonsense, lightweight, polarised pair for driving that stays in the car; and a second pair for the beach, camping, going out or street parading. This pair transforms me into a Californian movie extra.

Thongs

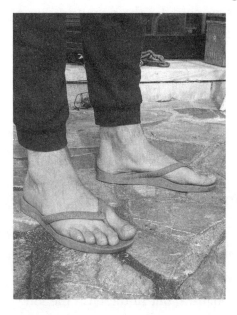

Like 'em or hate 'em, the ol' pluggers are now ubiquitous throughout our broad and sun-drenched land. Once derided by the lace-up and slip-on crowd, thongs have gained acceptance at the flashiest pubs and nosh pits everywhere – well, in Australia, anyway.

Gone are the crossed-out-thong stickers on doorways warning guests that exposed toes were an offence punishable by eviction. Now the Japanese-inspired flip-flops can be seen and heard echoing down the marble corridors of the finest establishments known to larrikins everywhere.

But there's a new foot holder that may be floor-slapping its way to dominance and heralding the old thong's demise. A revolutionary step that has podiatrists going broke through lack of foot-troubled clients, it's called the arch-support thong.

Various brands of this tenderfoot have established toeholds in chemists everywhere. I'm an arch believer in these curved-sole foot cushions and rarely wear anything else. They go particularly well with budgies, but, fellas, don't ever be seen wearing socks with thongs unless it's an emergency, or your fashion advisor might just give you the boot.

If you're looking for some toe protection, but want to stay light and airy, you might want to consider the ugly duckling of footwear: the Crocs. Invented in 2002 by three Americans, these reptilian foot dwellers are being snapped up globally and have rapidly become the go-to not-quite-a-shoe for boaties, fishers and outdoor types on the hunt for comfort. Friends swear by them, but if you like to show off your cute pedicure, thongs are still one step ahead on the style front.

Getting shirty

Shirts are a matter of practicality over style. The no-shirt or singlet look is a welcome mat for nasty cancerous blotches. T-shirts are fine, and come with every kind of logo and free corporate advertising known to multinationalism, but in the bush the long-sleeve with chest pockets is the go. When you're out in the dinghy for hours on end or find yourself without any shade or things have cooled down, simply roll down the sleeves and, bingo, you've got sun protection or added warmth right there.

The pockets allow you to store your mobile, box of matches or lost treasure map, leaving your hands free to do whatever the hell they like. The press-studded, long-sleeve pocketed shirt will give you the added advantage of lightning-fast removal. This is particularly handy if you're a fighting man, as pointed out by my menswear store-owner friend in Winton. (When I asked him if he had any studded shirts he replied, 'Oh, you want a fightin' shirt!')

The bottom half

When active in the outdoors of Australia in the warmer months, you can pretty well get by with shorts. They'll keep you cooler and give you more mobility. Personally, I prefer the type you wear with a belt, but elastic pull-ups are great training for adult nappies down the track.

Swimwear

When it comes to swimwear, the gender gap is wider than an elephant's rear end. Men seem to be confined to long, knee-length baggy shorts known as board shorts, while women wear body-hugging and often cheek-revealing snippets of cloth that only just conceal their private parts and are outrageously expensive, but far more practical than the men's daggy sag bags.

Men's budgies make much more sense and seem to go with the winter swimmers and clubbies, but for some strange reason they attract the ire of society. Go the boyleg: they're comfortable, modest, don't weigh you down, dry quickly and are bound to impress, from North Bondi to Broome.

CROCS, KAVA AND THE WARUMPI BAND SHOOT

Alice Springs and Galiwinku, January 1993

As mentioned, preparation is the mother of a successful bush trip. It doesn't mean being anal about every move and detail. It's just about having your shit together before you head out the door – like checking your camping gear, getting the car serviced, researching when and where to go and what the weather's going to be doing. Book ahead if need be, to take the anxiety out of having no place to stay and being forced to sleep in your car.

This story is a classic example of how leaving things to chance can end in disaster. Locals are usually comfortable in their familiar environs, but as a visitor, it can be challenging, to say the least.

My move to Alice Springs in 1981 proved to be a good one. After working at a government-funded resource centre, then helping to establish the first Aboriginal TV unit at the Central Australian Aboriginal Media Association (CAAMA), it became time to go out on my own. So, in about 1988, I established my very own television production company in Alice Springs. My office was right on the main drag of Todd Street Mall. This was my base, where I housed all my production gear and a U-matic video edit suite. Today the video machines, monitors and dubbing racks have given way to the computer, where you can do the lot and distribute directly to the boundless world of the web.

While much of my time was spent 'out bush' shooting videos in remote Aboriginal communities, there was the occasional job that happened in town. One of those was a photo shoot for a major fashion brand.

A series of faxes and phone calls preceded the arrival of a small army of Germans at my humble studio: a stylist, a make-up person, two gents from a Berlin advertising company, two camera assistants and the highly talented, loud and bossy fashion photographer who for the purposes of this story I'll call Konrad.

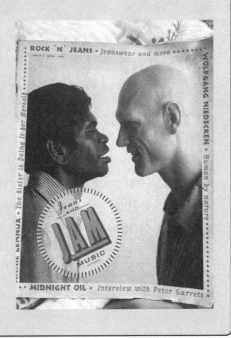

They were shooting stills for the fashion brand and wanted random people as talent. There was a flash pair of jeans and a shirt on offer, plus a $100 fee, so there were plenty of takers. All I had to do was go downstairs to the mall, recruit familiar faces, take them back upstairs, subject them to the make-up artist and stylist, then stand them in front of a big roll of paper under an assortment of lights. Konrad would go into contortions and acrobatic poses to get the picture just right, and then they were on their way – immortalised in jeans they could never afford with a $100 note in the pocket.

After a day or two of the shutter shenanigans, I informed the fashionistas that I had to go bush on a shoot for the now legendary filmmaker Rachel Perkins. Her first documentary production, the film was to meet and follow the various members of the Warumpi Band, an Aboriginal group with a white singer-guitarist from the central Australian community of Papunya. They were pioneers in writing and performing songs in an Aboriginal language, in this case Luritja, and were hugely popular throughout Aboriginal Australia. They reached a certain level of fame when they toured England and Europe. The mainstays and founders of the band is Luritja/Warlpiri man Sammy Butcher and his brothers.

EARLY ABORIGINAL BANDS IN CENTRAL OZ

Like much of Aboriginal Australia, the towns and communities around central Australia have produced their fair share of musicians and bands. A distinguishing feature of the music of the desert dwellers is the use of boomerangs and clap sticks that have accompanied the

The original members of Warumpi Band, less George, Papunya Town Hall, Northern Territory 1978.

cyclical singing of the Jukurrpa for many thousands of years. Guitars came along with the missionaries, and country-and-western music came along with just about everyone else. Before long, local stages hosted guitar-strumming performers like Gus Williams, Issac Yama (father of well-known performer Frank Yama), Herby Laughton and Bob Randall, to name a few.

When electric guitars hit the scene, whole bands emerged from the dust from far-flung communities.

In the late seventies my brother, Philip Batty, along with John Macumba and Freda Thornton (mother of celebrated filmmaker Warwick Thornton) established the first Aboriginal-owned and run radio station in Alice Springs under an umbrella organisation, the Central Australian Aboriginal Media Association (CAAMA). Soon CAAMA developed a terrestrial network that would deliver CAAMA radio far and wide throughout the desert communities.

CAAMA Radio staff, Alice Springs, Northern Territory 1983.

With an increased demand to feed the airwaves with local artists and in language, CAAMA started recording bands for the first time, including the now famous Warumpi Band from Papunya. Other bands quickly followed, such as Ilkari Maru from Amata in South Australia, Lajamanu Teenage Band and Areyonga Desert Tigers, as well as solo artists, choirs and groups that emerged from just about every desert community. Battle of the bands became a highlight of sports weekends and an opportunity for fledgling musicians to get on stage.

Today, Aboriginal bands have proliferated, with many getting a gig at the annual Bush Bands Bash in Alice Springs, attracting huge crowds who come to see their countrymen perform in some of the many central Australian languages.

Rachel's shoot was to start at Pupunya with the Butcher brothers, then head up to Arnhem Land in the Top End to film the flamboyant singer George Rrurrambu at his outstation island homeland near Elcho Island.

When I explained this to Konrad, he wanted in! He wanted to be the stills guy on the shoot. I didn't like his chances of coming on board, but I ran the idea past Rachel anyway.

'German stills guy, huh?' she responded quizzically.

'He wants to bring his stylist as well,' I said.

'Great. We need stills,' she said. 'So long as they pay their own way and we own the pics.'

We headed to Papunya. My role as the camera operator also meant organising the shoot, and Rachel brought along a sound engineer who resembled an international supermodel. Being January, it was going to be hot, so I organised lunch and downtime around midday and shooting through the cooler parts of day. It all went smoothly – plenty of tucker, cool drinks, swags, guitars around the fire ... Konrad and the stylist were in Ozzie outback heaven.

Next we flew from Alice to Darwin, then by small plane along the coast of Arnhem Land to the small Aboriginal community of what was then called Elcho Island, now known by its Yolngu name, Galiwinku. It was a fairly typical Arnhem Land community – slow-paced and relaxed. Coconut palms lined the water's edge and family groups sauntered along with spears and their day's catch. This was where my organising finished and we went freestyle.

We were here to hang out with George, the lead singer of the Warumpi Band. The idea was to go to his island outstation with his family and film him on his country hunting, fishing, dancing – all the usual Arnhem Land stuff.

George met us at the airstrip and took us into the community. Shirtless kids with big toothy smiles waved to us as we made our way to George's father's place in the back of a ute. All we needed was a boat big enough to take our crew, gear, swags, George, his brother, half a dozen ladies and a few kids out to George's island outstation some distance from Galiwinku.

Our quest to find a boat big enough was stymied, not by a lack of boats, but by a lack of organising. Then we spotted an older Yolngu man who had just pulled a decent-sized boat into his driveway and was hosing it out in slowmo. It was a six-metre aluminium dinghy with the roof torn off and a hefty inboard-outboard motor on the back.

George approached the boat owner and filled him in on our mission: to get all of us and our gear to his outstation. The man was delighted to take us for a doable fee and fuel. His glazed eyes and slow smile were the result of a heavy night on the kava (kava is legal and not considered a disruptive influence in Top End communities). This didn't seem to worry George. We were to meet him on the other side of the island; he'd fuel up and meet us there in halfa.

I was used to running my own show, but being a desert rat, I was off country and not so familiar with Top End protocols and the ways of the Yolngu.

Typical coastline around Galiwinku, Northern Territory.

Naturally, though, I had a few queries for George as the afternoon was approaching the three o'clock mark.

'How far out to your island?' I asked casually as we waited on the banks.

'Not really far,' he replied simply.

'Should we buy some tucker?'

'Nah, we blackfellas, mate, and this our Country,' he said confidently. 'Plenty tucker out there.'

Partly satisfied with this, I waited with George for the old man and his boat.

When the old man arrived, I was surprised he'd not only filled the boat's fuel tanks, but also a 44-gallon drum on deck as well. *Hmm, why do we need all this fuel?* I wondered.

The boat was backed into the water and loaded with us, our gear and a Toyota-full of George's family. Their total possessions consisted of a guitar and two spears. We were off!

George Rrurrambu prior to being shipwrecked,
Galiwinku, Northern Territory.

As we zoomed along a wide channel fringed with thick, dark mangroves, the Germans were transported into a blissful state of awe and wonder. While Konrad had the foresight to bring a hat, the stylist stood up and pushed his face into the warm rushing air. His shirt was off, and a crimson-and-gold scarf was flying in his raised hand like a flowing flag of freedom.

'Konraddd!' he yelled joyously over the huge screaming motor. 'We are in middle of nowhere!'

Konrad's ear-to-ear smile and nod affirmed the stylist's excitement and ever-increasing wind- and sunburn.

After we'd been full-bore for an hour, the channel opened to a kilometre-wide mouth and then the open sea. The old man throttled down and we bobbed close to the shoreline of some nearby land. The sun had just about given up for the day and, with no island in sight, I asked George where his island home was.

'See that dot?'

He pointed into the distance. On the horizon I could just make out a tiny speck of land.

'But the sun's about to go down,' I said apprehensively. 'It'll be dark by the time we get there!'

'We'll be right, mate.'

That unsettling feeling of impending disaster started in my gut then quickly rose to my rational mind. Just what the hell were we doing?

Rachel seemed a lot calmer, exuding a 'this mob know what they're doing' demeanour. The Germans seemed totally absorbed in the moment, the present company, the scenery and the adventure, and were exchanging gee-whiz dialogue in chuckling German. Were my sensory alarm bells going off prematurely?

The choppy water and heavy breeze of the open ocean was slowly pushing us closer to a rocky headland. As we tossed up what we were going to do, the motor cut out.

We were now at the mercy of the choppy seas, wind and deepening furrows between ocean swells. The old man cranked the motor to no avail then, as calm as a sea cucumber, smiled at us.

'That motor hungry for fuel.'

Stating the obvious was little help given our predicament. To make things worse, a razor-sharp reef was becoming visible under the boat, and a crashing shoreline was just metres away.

In desperation, George and his brother jumped overboard in a vain attempt to push the heavily rising and falling lump of aluminium away from the reef and rocky shoreline.

Meanwhile, the old man gave up cranking the outboard and signalled that we needed to get fuel from the 44-gallon drum into the boat's tank.

Waves were now sloshing over the side of the dinghy, and the women and kids were not happy. The youngest ones were broadcasting their screams to all aboard, who were hanging on for their lives.

While being tossed about like ping-pong balls in a washing machine, the Germans and I managed to rock-and-roll the 44-gallon drum towards the fuel intake on top of the gunwale, wondering how we'd get the petrol in the impossibly small hole without spilling most of it. The still-smiling old man dug out an old hand-crank fuel pump, which we soon learnt had seized up a few decades ago. Then he handed us a length of 2-inch hose, which wouldn't fit in the mouth of the drum. In desperation and with superhuman strength, we lifted the drum and managed to slosh a few cups of fuel into the fuel-tank inlet.

By now the boat was seriously scraping the reef and drifting closer to the crashing shoreline. The boys in the water were doing their best, but as the boat rose over the next peaking wave, so did they, clinging fruitlessly onto the side of the boat.

The boat was powered by an inboard-outboard motor, which meant the propeller shaft could be raised out of the water to prevent it hitting the bottom while the motor could run independently. The old man had the presence of mind to lift the propeller out of the water while he kept cranking the motor. Eventually the motor rumbled and revved back to life.

'Get in and get us out of here!' I yelled to George in the water.

The trough of the next wave nearly cracked the hull wide open as it connected with jagged rocks below. It washed George over the stern and onto the floor of the boat. He leapt up, brushed the old man aside and took to the controls. In a frenzy he pushed the button to lower the outboard part of the motor into the water and hit the throttle. At that moment we rose up on the biggest wave of the day and the rear of the boat went down deep, but with the motor screaming and the propeller at full pelt, we just managed to rise over the top of the wave and smash down the other side, saved from certain disaster.

But the following tsunami showed us who was who. When the rear went down again the propeller hit the bottom and snapped the shear pin that kept the drive shaft connected and the propeller turning. Screams and yells of desperation heralded an angel who momentarily quelled the angry sea and sent a lull between the breakers that allowed us to gently rise up, down and away.

As if by a miracle, the boat was moving ever so slowly forward with the motor at full revs. With the shear pin broken, it meant the drive shaft was not turning the propeller as it should, but provided just enough grip to move us inch by inch away from the waves, the rocks and the likely drowning of all on board.

Exhausted and wet, and with the light fading, we chugged our way back into the channel and pulled up at a quiet cove with a placid beach. We silently unloaded the boat and collapsed on the sand. This was before the invention of mobile phones, and with no radio or flares we were as stuck as a buffalo in mud. The motor on the boat didn't have enough guts to take us anywhere and was abandoned. Everyone wandered off to one of two camps: us and the Germans, or George and his family. We quietly got fires going, stretched out on the sand, meditated on our near-death experience then gave in to our heavily sunburnt eyelids.

The next day we tossed around rescue scenarios until the idea of being found faded, along with our memories of cold beer, comfy beds and, above all, food. We were in the height of the unbearably hot wet season, with humidity you could cut with a machete. The bush at the back of the beach was impenetrable, crocs were eyeing us off from the water's edge, and the mozzies and sandflies could almost carry you away. On the upside, everywhere you dug on the steep little beach made a pool of brown but perfectly drinkable water.

Luckily, George and his family had been busy hunting for food, which amounted to several stingrays and a pile of oysters the size of plates.

On the second night of camp *Survivor*, Rachel's glamorous sound engineer realised that she and Konrad were cosmically and spiritually connected through their prior devotion to Bhagwan Shree Rajneesh, the leader of the orange-clad cult-like Rajneesh religious order. Thanks to this shared higher-order consciousness, the pair, along with the stylist, decided now was as good a time as any to crack open a jar of preserved magic mushrooms the Germans had miraculously acquired during their travels. Managing to restrain myself from the ingestion of mind-altering fungi, I now had to endure the terrified trio as they imagined crocodiles crawling towards our cluster of swags and saw coloured balls and flashes in the sky, none of which was helpful.

By day three, the stylist had broken out in a nasty sunburn rash and Konrad was plotting our escape plan.

'David,' he said, frenzied, 'we leave the others here and take the boat to the other side of the channel.'

'And then what?' I replied.

'We get help.'

'From ... ?'

My lack of enthusiasm for his plan brought on a full-blown hissy fit.

'We must get off this place!' Konrad cried. 'I need to get to Sydney! I have an appointment with Peter Garrett in two days!'

'Bugger,' I muttered in faux sympathy. 'Don't see that happening.'

Day four, and the novelty of oyster steaks and roasted stingray balls was wearing thin. There was no sign of being rescued and no likelihood of it. As much as I wanted to get out of our predicament, I had to work on just staying calm. To survive being stuck in the desert is one thing, but getting off a croc- and mosquito-infested island in the middle of a remote and isolated coast in the height of the wet season had me stumped.

I approached George, who seemed unfazed by the events and almost seemed to think it was situation normal.

'The Germans really need to get to Sydney,' I said.

'Okay, we sail back,' he said. 'Two o'clock today.'

It was as if he'd known how to get off the island all along, but was enjoying being on home ground.

With little ceremony, he smashed his way into the thick scrub and came back with some long, thin saplings. He asked me for sheets from my swag, and some wire and gaffer tape from my kit bag. In no time he'd fashioned a fold-out Macassan-type sail, the ones that look like a big V.

Rachel Perkins with George Rrurrambu holding makeshift sail that got us home, Galiwinku, Northern Territory.

When everyone was back in the boat, George lashed the sail to the front. Then our Yolngu companions pushed us out into the middle of the channel with little fuss. But the poor Germans had had enough, and grizzled away in their native tongue. I was also pretty annoyed that the whole event had happened, but Rachel was cool, calm and content.

At around 2 pm, as if by magic and just as George had predicted, a gentle breeze hit our faces. It became stronger. I will never forget what the Yolngu call that lifesaving wind – murai yil yil. The breeze grew solid, consistently pushing against our swag sail. We slowly cruised back up the channel using the useless outboard as a rudder. At about 8 pm, we pulled up at the little beach on the other side of Elcho Island.

George and his Yolngu family were totally unfazed. In fact, they seemed to have enjoyed the whole experience, laughing and joking as they climbed onto the tray of a ute that belonged to a relation fishing nearby. For them, they'd got to hang out on their Country for a few days, hunt and eat as much stingray and monster oysters as they liked, and have some good ol' family togetherness, including a few fireside singalongs.

But a dark cloud hung over the rest of us. The Germans had become solemn and demanding; Rachel and the sound engineer were quiet and subdued; I was just totally over the entire situation. To make things worse, we all had serious sunburn. We looked like Hiroshima survivors. Luckily the concierge from the five-star resort up the road sent a limo to take us to our air-conditioned, king-sized luxury apartments, and put on a banquet to die for – in our dreams!

No: instead, we waited in the dark by a mangrove-fringed beach, swatting sandflies and mozzies for what seemed forever, feeling like washed-up refugees that the world had turned its back on. Then it started raining.

Word must have got out in the community that we needed to be picked up, because eventually a pair of dim headlights emerged from the gloom. A ute pulled up, and once we'd climbed on the tray with our gear it lurched back up the track to the community.

Elcho Island at that time was a hotel-free destination, which is okay if you're a day visitor, but if you're five unexpected survivors of a holiday in hell needing care, comfort and food, forget about it. The only place the ute driver could think to accommodate us was the veranda of the local primary school. We were dropped off at the school, dark, wet, hungry and not happy. Konrad launched into a tirade about missing his appointment with Peter Garrett in Sydney while the stylist nodded vigorously. 'Ja! Ja!' I was beyond over it and in a mute state of catatonia. After a while, I dragged myself down to the end of the veranda and rolled out my swag, only to be reminded that my sheets had been commandeered as emergency sails. Steaming hot, sunburnt and lying on raw foam rubber, all I wanted was to be out of there, but eventually I nodded off.

We flew out first thing in the morning.

We never got to George's outstation, but I did manage to film him on Country while we were stranded, and got enough material to satisfy Rachel and her bosses at SBS.

A week or so later, we filmed the Warumpi Band's first-ever recording session in Sydney with the rest of the group, including Neil Murray and Allen Murphy on drums.

The Germans rescheduled their meeting with Peter Garrett and Midnight Oil, and invited Rachel, the sound engineer, George and me to the most expensive restaurant in Sydney. Needless to say, nobody ordered the oysters.

Following our *Survivor* reunion dinner, we all went up to the Germans' penthouse suite at the top of the Shangri-La Hotel at Circular Quay, where bottles of French champagne were waiting. We lolled about, intoxicated by the views, laughingly recalling moments from our boat trip to hell.

Then Konrad gripped my shoulder.

'David, that trip was so much fun,' he said earnestly. 'I would like to come with you again ...'

5

HITTING THE ROAD

Most years around May or June I like to pack my swag and hit the road north. By then, the ocean along the New South Wales south coast has gone cold and the veggie garden is taking a nap. It's a good excuse to check in on my kids and grandkids in Broome and Alice Springs. Plus, as the south coast goes into hibernation the north comes alive.

I prepare for a few months before I go. This time I was taking a postie motorbike to leave in Broome so when I flew up I'd have wheels to get around town, and the kids could use it when I wasn't there. I'd also bolted a solar panel onto the roof of my ute, with battery and inverter to run a fridge, small 240-volt appliances and lighting.

I don't like spending weeks behind the wheel alone, so I always try to find one or two willing travel buddies. This time I was heading to Broome with two female friends, Narelle and Carol, via the Nullarbor and Western Australia's coastline.

Narelle was a fellow bushwalker, a seasoned bushy from way back and a good mate. Her competency in the bush was second to none. She was also a cheerful minimalist who needed few comforts, had lived in wild places in handmade bush shacks, meditated, gave great massages and practised yoga most days.

Carol was a good friend's little sister. She'd never slept in a swag and wasn't a camper. But she had a wicked sense of humour, and needed a break. Besides, travelling with a partner is one thing, but with mates, it's better in threes.

Both Carol and Narelle jumped at the suggestion of a drive to Broome, even though they hardly knew each other. Why wouldn't they – they had a top-class guide, a reliable vehicle fully fitted out and spare time.

My VW Amarok twin cab has a custom-made canopy and a roof rack built for heavy loads and doubles as a filming platform. A second spare wheel on a trip around Oz is a must, and that was going on the roof with the postie bike. The canopy had canvas roll-up sides for easy access to all parts of the tub and I'd screwed metal sheeting on the tailgate to use as the kitchen bench.

So it was Broome or bust, and another big adventure. It was time to hit the road!

Now *you've* got your travelling arrangements sorted, the pets organised, and the house locked and bolted, it's time to go bush. Just in case you've been too preoccupied to think things through before your foot hits the pedal, here's a handy checklist:

- Sort who or what is going to water your garden or plants.
- Make sure your vehicle is in good order, and service it beforehand if it's near its due date.
- Pack some cash – whole towns can lose internet, leaving cash the only option.
- Ensure all equipment, including tyre-changing gear, is checked and on board.
- Check tyre pressure, along with everything under the hood.
- Make sure everything is secure and tied down.
- Check mobile-phone charging leads and adaptors are on board.
- Double- and triple-check tow ball, towing hitches and rear lights.
- Download audiobooks, podcasts or music - mobile reception is patchy out there.
- Grab a map book – you may not always be in range for maps on the mobile.

Now you're ready to hit the road.

Packed and ready as I can be for a trip around Oz.

Girt by dirt – the wide open road

When you're out on the road it's always nice to have a destination in mind, whether it's for the end of the day, a week's time or a grand finale for a year-long drive around our big island. Driving aimlessly is not only a gas-guzzling waste of time, but a missed opportunity to experience the satisfaction of arriving somewhere.

If you've set your sights on a long-distance drive, chances are you'll take on all kinds of roads and road surfaces. Mostly, it's a case of applying common sense, but sometimes a good sense of driving isn't that common. So, here are a few tips.

The single strip of tar

As you head into more remote areas, you may get to the point where the usual dual-lane bitumen road narrows down to a single-car-width strip of bitumen. On both sides of the black strip, it's well-worn dirt in various states of smoothness, from baby's bum to potholes to bone-rattling corrugations. This is all fine as you cruise along at a reasonable 80–100 kilometres per hour, but when you encounter a vehicle coming in the opposite direction you're going to have to share the thin black strip. The concept of slowing down at this point can often elude the less courteous driver as they hurtle along with their driver-side wheels on the bitumen while the passenger side smashes down onto the unsealed stuff, showering rocks, gravel and dirt straight at the oncoming vehicle. These people are often referred to as 'dickheads'. A much better idea is for both cars to slow right down and gently pass each other with a friendly smile, wave and an intact windscreen.

If you find yourself on bitumen rivulets, it's probable it carries trucks, road trains and tour buses. In this case, it's in your interest to slow down when you encounter one of these beasts, pull up and let the rock-throwing monster have the entire black strip. This will also ensure you're not engulfed in a voluminous cloud of dust, which may obscure your vision and set you on a course into an oncoming vehicle and a fatal head-on collision.

Bone-rattling corrugations.

The ups and downs of unsealed roads

Australia has its fair share of dirt roads. Some are even called highways. They come in a variety of states and surfaces. A well-maintained and freshly graded dirt road can be as smooth as claypan after rain. A dirt road that hasn't been visited by the road-maintenance gang for a while can be a corrugated nightmare.

Some travellers are daunted by the chassis shakers and think the way to handle them is to slow down to 30 or 40 kilometres per hour. This is a bad idea. To witness a car crawling along with passengers under the influence of corrugations is like watching a god-fearing cult whip each other with thorn branches.

The tried-and-true technique to avoid premature births, spinal injuries and severe damage to the chariot is to get up to 80 kilometres per hour and cruise. Some say the frequency of the corrugations is created by the repetitive up and down movement of cars' and trucks' suspension. Another widely held belief is that if you drive on the wrong side of the road, the effect of the corrugations diminishes. I've tried this hundreds of times and am yet to be convinced.

DESERT ELDERS MAKING ROADS IN SAND HILL COUNTRY

My own desert-road-making story goes back to 1982, when I accompanied a small group of five Ngaanyatjarra men (four of whom had met white people for the first time only ten years earlier), a surveyor and the anthropologist Ushma Scales into the Gibson Desert in Western Australia, about as remote as it gets. The task was to film the survey work for the roads needed for seismic exploration for the Shell oil company.

This may sound like a nasty exercise in destroying the ancestral lands of the Ngaanyatjarra, but the Elders had a rock-solid co-partnership deal with Shell, and the Elders were pleased as punch that roads were being made on their Country, as they'd give them better access to sacred sites, ceremonially important places and, most importantly, involve putting down water bores so they could build new communities and outstations.

The leader of the traditional owners was Andrew Lawson, a man who grew up in the mission at Warburton. Andrew was called on when any matters of cultural sensitivity or regarding sacred sites required his input. But he was also skilled in the art of water divining, and he saved the oil company thousands of dollars in test drilling. Andrew would tell the company where to drill and *bingo*, he'd be on the money every time. It was a joy to watch him at work. On this trip, Andrew was the driver of the tray-back Toyota four-wheel-drive truck and general assistant to the other men, who knew the country like others might know their backyard. We travelled out way past the community of Warburton to a distant oil-exploration camp.

Our team had the job of heading out in front of the graders and bulldozers to mark where the new seismic roads should or shouldn't go. The Ngaanyatjarra crew's job was to inform the surveyor where it was okay to build the new roads, avoiding sacred sites, burial areas, rock holes or any other places of significance.

At one point we were in what's known as the 'breakaway country', which is full of long lines of small cliffs. We would survey up to the edge of a breakaway, then work out a way to drive down it, then drive another 20 kilometres to the next breakaway. At one breakaway, Mr Jennings (all the Warburton mob were Mr this or Mrs that) called me over and told me to follow him down the face of a breakaway to a large cave overhang. Via broken English and my small understanding of Ngaanyatjarra, he explained we were in a 'wet-time' camp, a cave where he and his family had been camping just ten years prior like they had for thousands of years. He pointed out spear-sharpening grooves, an old fireplace and the bones of animals they'd eaten the last time they were camped there. It was a grounding insight via a first-hand account into a desert nomad's way of life and the harsh but beautiful lives they led before meeting the white man.

The way the survey work was conducted was straightforward. The surveyor would look through his theodolite, which was like a telescope, and pick a distant tree or rock. Andrew and his men would look through it too, then drive in a straight line to the spot and radio through. The surveyor would then move to that spot and leave marker pegs where the road was to go.

Typical sand dunes, Great Sandy Desert, Western Australia.

But when we came to thick sandhill country, the operation took an amazing turn. Nature had created a maze of low sand dunes. Traversing them took hours of up and down and reversing. When faced with this, the men would look through the theodolite, identify the distant sand dune and drive off, weaving up and down and back and forth on their way. Meanwhile we'd light a fire, boil the billy, throw on a few T-bones wrapped in foil (which were regularly dropped by plane on our tucker-drop days) and sit back while we waited for Andrew to call us on the radio and signal with a mirror where he was.

An hour or two later:

'Kulini! Kulini! Wati Tjuta Kulini Nyalu nininyi kuwari ... Kulini!'

Which roughly translates to: 'Can you hear me! Can you hear me! All you men there. We're sitting at that place now.'

Going by their knowledge and innate sense of direction, Andrew and his men had driven to the exact spot and were now waiting for us. It was such an incredible feat, and once again an earthly reminder of whose Country we were on and how well they knew it.

Deadly dust

If you're driving on a dirt road, fine dust is an annoying inevitability. Unless some moisture has settled it or turned it into mud, it's going to be there, no matter what. When the dust gets as fine as talcum powder and as deep as snow it's called 'bulldust'. When it's even finer it's known as 'fugitive dust'. This occurs when there's insufficient moisture content in the ground to hold the soil together.

Bulldust can conceal deep potholes and rocks and clog up the air filter on your vehicle, causing damage and increasing fuel consumption. There's not much you can do to avoid it, but unless you have X-ray vision, never attempt to overtake a car that's spewing out blinding clouds of dust behind it. Even on the remotest roads, you never know when a car might be coming the other way just as you're overtaking the dust maker. This is especially the case with trucks and road trains. Rather than stew behind the wheel waiting for the wind to change, the truck to pull over, or a sudden strip of bitumen to materialise, lift your foot and pull over for a while.

ROAD KILL

An often-unavoidable obstacle while driving our vast network of country roads and highways is an animal. One way to minimise the carnage *and* the damage to your front end or, even worse, rolling your vehicle, is to avoid driving from dusk to dawn altogether.

Kangaroos, wombats, emus and feral animals love roaming about in search of green grass or pools of water by the road. If you must go nocturnal, slow down and make sure you have enough lights onboard to see what's up ahead and don't swerve too hard. A high percentage of vehicle casualties and deaths are caused when a driver swerved and lost control. If you do kill something, move it way off the road, as birds of prey, like wedge-tail eagles, will be attracted to the fresh kill and become the next victims.

Driving etiquette

Most of us motorists are accustomed to being Courteous Law-Abiding Drivers, or CLADS.

As CLADS, we inhabit the space behind the steering wheel and go about operating pedals and switches in a responsible manner while navigating our way to a destination, usually in the company of other CLADS doing the same thing. By far, the majority of this activity happens in urban areas amidst a system of sealed bitumen carriageways, and involves a high level of compliance and anonymity – unless a CLAD encounters a Reckless Angry Dangerous Driver, or RADD, in a metal-on-metal interaction, and they get to meet each other in a usually heightened state of shock and confusion, by the side of the road, at the hospital or in the courtroom.

When CLADS leave their urban habitats and navigate their chariots to the extremities of our big backyard, there are a few unwritten rural and remote road-etiquette guidelines that, if followed correctly, will elevate their standing to Outback CLAD (OCLAD), initiating them into the fellowship and camaraderie of long-distance and outback drivers right across Australia.

Communication

On the wide-open road, we are a community of like-minded distance devotees, with the driver compulsorily gripping the wheel of destiny with eyes scanning what's ahead. Steering the ship can be a lonely mesmeric meditation, but sometimes you can connect with fellow mesmerists coming in the opposite direction. In simple finger talk, you can convey your inner thoughts and feelings to the oncoming human.

The finger wave

Rather than winding down the window and letting in flies, bugs, heat, dust, noise or humidity, the driver can deploy the finger wave, a simple gesture performed with one or both hands while still firmly gripping the wheel as you tear along at 100 kilometres per hour. The timing of the wave is critical; the more it is in sync with the oncoming driver, the stronger the message transferred.

Eye contact makes for a deeper connection, but is not critical. It is important that the other driver is not out of sight before you engage in any form of non-physical contact, or you will have wasted your time and expectation.

The finger wave is a nuanced gesture with many variations, and can only be performed by the driver. Here are some of the innumerable variations. Practise and learn.

Gesture	Meaning
Right index finger raised	G'day, how ya goin?
Both index fingers raised	Hey, I'm cool and so are you.
Double index with pursed lips	G'day, love ya rig.
Double index, lips and raised brows	Hey, mate, dunno about the buff horns on ya bull bar.
Five-finger raise, both hands	So pleased to see ya. Hasn't been another car for yonks.
All fingers, both hands and brows	Wow, we both got the same kind of car.
Thumbs up	[Obsolete due to overuse or possible misunderstanding.]

The nod

At times, especially after a few days of finger waving, it's okay to just respond to the oncoming finger wave with a nod. Any giver of the digit will totally understand and lower the greeting finger with the self-assurance of having at least tried. A grimacing nod is like a slap in the face to an oncoming comrade, and is usually performed when tired and emotional. It can have a few meanings:

- Look ... I'm over the finger waves right now!
- Yeah ... big deal ... so I'm the only other car you've seen all day.
- Mate ... I'll say g'day, but really, your car is a piece of junk.

The wink

The wink is a bold move and is only pulled out in response to the other driver winking, in the case of prior familiarity or to acknowledge a shared experience. If none of these situations apply, it's best avoided, as the other driver may take it as amorous intent.

Driving speed

Distressed drivers can be a danger to not only themselves but every other person anywhere near or on a road. You don't have to be a Buddhist to be kind, thoughtful and courteous. Drivers can achieve this by being mindful of a few simple driver failings.

Move over, Rover

Even the mildest mannered, most easygoing CLAD will have their boundaries stretched to breaking point by a crawler. There's nothing inherently wrong with trying to break your personal best fuel-saving record from Mount Isa to Camooweal, but not everyone is on your team. Save your followers for Facebook or Instagram, and let the normal speedsters queued up behind you go free. Pull over and acknowledge the gratitude of the passing motorcade with a smile and a wave, then hop into the van and have a cuppa, or break out the thesaurus and solve that pesky crossword clue your partner has been stuck on all morning.

Back orf, buddy

A universal pest and definitely in the RADD category is the tailgater. The brain is a wondrous thing, a complexity of micro switches, grey matter that is responsible for all our emotions and reactions – the list goes on. Various parts of the brain can be trained to better deal with things like anxiety, loss or betrayal, or can be enhanced to gain greater insights into philosophy or things of wonder. The brain is a cavernous receptacle of endless self-development.

So while the brain is a thing of wonder, it's an even bigger wonder how and why it can guide the tailgater to tailgate. It's a pursuit worthy of the dumbest-thing-in-the-world prize. The practice not only precipitates severe road rage by the tailgated, but encourages risk-taking behaviours such as near-death overtaking attempts. It's also a sure winner for diminishing the tailgater's brake pads.

CAR GAMES

After a week on the road, you're podcasted out, you've told all your near-death survival stories, played I Spy and Spotto, and you've still got a week to go on the blacktop. I faced this dilemma on a recent drive across the country. The further north my travel companions and I got, the more vans we were sitting behind or overtaking. We became fascinated by the names that the van manufacturers chose to describe their dream machines. They were obviously invented to evoke a smug response from the owners towing them and envy from the vanless nomads looking on.

So, in our little four-wheel cocoon, we would spot a new van name then try to interpret just what the names were meant to convey.

Name	Meaning
Apache	Horse-drawn and free spirited
Australia	True-blue dinky-di, with Southern Cross cushion covers
Big Red	Indulge your inner couch potato
Blue Sky	Infinite travels into an unknown universe
Cavalier	Bold and brash interloper
Coachman	Gender-specific solo touring
Concept	Released way too early

Condor	Soaring high above all other vans
Conqueror	Always gets the best-powered van site – or else
Crusader	Conquering all highways and camping grounds that come before it
Elite	You will feel superior to all other van owners
Hard Korr	Rugged individuals ready to take on serious adventures but unable to spell
Kokoda	Tough, rugged, go anywhere to defend the faith of caravanners everywhere
New Age Manta	Touring manta ray yoga teachers
Star Craft	Spaceship interior with float chamber
Stirling	Can only be bought with silver
Royal Flare	Fake gold paintwork
New Generation	Loves going to festivals; must be purchased with crypto
The Odyssey	Guaranteed to always get you back Homer
Ovation	Gets a round of applause as it enters every caravan park
Regal	Royal coach with indoor throne
Regent	Base-line royalty

Retreat	Indoor yoga and vegetarian sweat lodge
Silverline	Rough around the edges ... not quite gold
Skytrax	Spaced-out travelling
Summer Life	Only good for three months of the year
Supreme Spirit	Get on board for an out-of-body experience
Top Gun	Transforms into a jet fighter
Wild Cat	Feral, dreadlocked adventurers on board

Then there are the slogans written on the back of the vans.

Kiss the roses	At last we're free to enjoy our senior years, though it could be a thorny ride
Adventure before dementia	Speaks for itself
Comfort that follows you everywhere	Clever types on board

Trying to direct the *Black As* boys, featuring the semi-destroyed Suzuki Vitara, Ramingining, Northern Territory.

MORE BUSH CARS – AND BUSH MECHANICS – I HAVE KNOWN

Twenty years after making *Bush Mechanics* I found myself landing in a small single-engine aeroplane on a dirt airstrip on the outskirts of the Aboriginal community of Ramingining. I had answered a call from four young men who had grown up watching *Bush Mechanics* and wanted their own version of a show just like it, but in the wilds of Arnhem Land.

As is the way in this business, we needed to make a pilot to help raise interest in the new TV show and, above all, the dollars to make it. I stepped out of the plane and met four young men who would later become the now world-famous *Black As* boys: Jerome, Chico, Dino and Joe. We motored into the community and in no time we were down to business, discussing what we were going to do. I'd allowed the following day to do all the shooting for the pilot, then I'd fly home the day after that.

I suggested a hunting trip, but something that required no guns, as it might not win any friends in trying to raise the dollar. Fishing was out due to unfavourable tides, and hunting buffalo with spears might mean losing one or all of the boys to a flight to the nearest hospital. Surely there was something that required a journey in a car, jeopardy and near-death experiences, and resulted in traditional food from nature that everyone just loves to eat? Of course! Mangrove worms!

Next we needed a car, a bush basher that would last at least a day and present serious mechanical challenges.

 Watch Video:Making *Black As*

The Suzuki Vitara – the car that went to heaven

Suzi gets a traditional send off after the drowning incident.

On the morning of our one-day pilot shoot, we gathered out the front of Joe's house, ready for mangrove-worm action.

What about a car? By the side of the road where we were standing sat a dilapidated Suzuki Vitara – no wheels, no bonnet, an interior fully mulched and a tangle of multi-coloured wires strewn throughout the sad-looking motor that had been exposed to more than its fair share of wet seasons. With our shoot day ticking away, the boys dispersed then reappeared with a battery and a collection of wheels. I held as much hope for the poor little Suzi engine ever pushing a piston again as I did a brand-new Toyota falling from the sky.

But wheels were coerced onto the remaining studs, the seats were cleared of a few wheelie bins of debris and a battery was plonked next to the motor. Joe and Chico emerged as the mechanical brains of the foursome, and set about pulling out various wires, stripping off the plastic and twisting them together to see what would happen.

Then the two bush mechanics trickled petrol down the throat of the carby and cranked the motor. A ball of flame shot out the open carby throat, and the car returned to the land of the living, reincarnated as the star of a TV show that would entertain millions of YouTube and Facebook devotees the world over and carry the boys to international fame.

The Suzuki's first job was to transport the boys to get mangrove worms. Any other worm hunt would be pretty straightforward: drive to the nearest mangroves, navigate through a tangle of mangrove roots, chop a rotten bit of wood, pull out a few feet of worm and eat it. Job done. But hey – we were making a promo for an action-packed TV show, so we needed drama, suspense and ingenuity.

This was performed by the ute load. The little Suzi had to cross a croc-infested river on a makeshift log bridge, push its way through deep salty mud and burst through rings of flaming grass fires. After retrieving a few billy cans of worms, the Suzi had its ignition and steering lock smashed to oblivion with an axe, only to power on with renewed vitality, stronger and more determined than ever.

After just one day of filming madcap action, car destruction and mangrove-worm collecting, I had enough to make not one, but three rollicking, fun-filled five-minute pilots. And they smashed it. Broadcasters were scrambling to put their name on it, high-profile production companies wanted it, and the boys were an overnight sensation.

When I returned to Ramingining nine months later to shoot the series, the now legendary Suzuki was in an even worse state than before. Since we'd made the pilot, Ramingining had been hit head-on by a massive cyclone. Vast areas of bush had been trashed and flattened. Hunting tracks and even main roads were now impassable. The poor old Suzuki had been left with a flat tyre on one of those hunting tracks next to a massive tree that the cyclone uprooted and which fell right on top of poor old Suzi. It was perfect!

Straight up, the boys had to work out how to extract the crumpled mess, then get it going. Axes and tomahawks swung into action and in no time the uprights around the windscreen had been chopped off, the windscreen removed and the flat tyres replaced. We were back in action.

With the roads, hunting tracks and land-based action a no-go, our only option was to take to the water. A dinghy was borrowed and before long the cyclone-ravaged Suzi was merrily towing it along.

With Joe behind the wheel, the indestructible bush chariot was backing the dinghy into the water when it decided to create one of *Black As*'s most unforgettable moments. The boat and trailer pulled Suzi down a slippery, muddy bank and just kept going.

Joe abandoned ship and swam to shore as we watched our hero car sink deeper and deeper. Remarkably, the motor just kept running. As the car slid down into its murky grave, the noisy exhaust became a muted giant bubble machine, sending toxic puff balls to the surface. As its motoring life flashed before its steering wheel, the Suzi's open carby took a gulp of water and died, before slipping away peacefully to be at one with the crocs, mud crabs, sharks and mythical creatures of the deep. The only retrievable item was the battery, which Chico wasted no time in diving down to retrieve. He surfaced like a treasure hunter clutching a chest of gold medallions. All the while, the swirling waters of the nearby mangroves were rising higher, sending the beloved Suzi deeper into its watery grave.

Oblivious to the vehicular tragedy, the dinghy freed itself from the sunken trailer and floated off before it was secured to a mangrove bush. After all the drama, the boys took time out to light a fire, reflect on the passing of their old friend, cook some mud crabs and have a sleep, something which always comes easy.

We filmed a dozen or so more episodes around fishing, island exploring and spearing crocs before it was decided that it was bad form to just leave the Suzuki and trailer submerged on someone's traditional Country. It needed to be retrieved and put to rest.

The boys found a cyclone-trashed Hyundai and gave it another life. We drove to the muddy croc spot at low tide and used the Hyundai to pull out the Suzi. It took every valve-bouncing drop of engine power, but ol' Suzi and the boat trailer slowly slithered out of the deep mud and back to hard, dry land.

The car's hard-earned celebrity status, selflessness and ability to overcome almost insurmountable odds needed celebrating. It had gone above and beyond, and it was agreed unanimously that it deserved a proper send-off. A dignified cremation with all the Yolngu ceremonial trimmings was in order.

No longer able to get along under its own steam, the boys' old hunting mate was towed to an abandoned quarry. Here it was stroked affectionately with bunches of leaves, had hands laid on it and was revered as a one-in-a-million modacar that would live on in the hearts and minds of millions who knew her, as they watched her incredible feats of endurance on screens and mobile phones in every corner of the planet. Then the interior was stuffed with grass and leaves, and the car set on fire. As the flames started to rise, the boys retired to a nearby vantage point to watch and reflect.

'Well, it's gone to car heaven,' Joe said affectionately.

'Is there really a car heaven?' Dino asked.

Chico recounted all the places and good times Suzi had given them, including taking them on treacherous river crossings, on dozens of trips to Darwin and buffalo-hunting expeditions, and, above all, delivering them to the all-important secret world of men's business. It was a motoring life well spent.

Chico

'I'm not scared of you!' … Chico faces off his uncle Oppy in *Black As*.

Chico was born in a hospital in Nhulunbuy, north-east Arnhem Land. His family came from Ramingining, a remote Aboriginal community to the east of Nhulunbuy, and Chico grew up and went to school there. When he was ten, he moved onto his ancestral land at the outstation community of Yathalamarra a few kilometres up the road. He is a fully initiated law man, and has been entrusted with the knowledge, understanding and cultural responsibilities of his Yolngu countrypeople. Chico is also a fully trained health worker and a gun bush mechanic.

Chico speaks: 'My dad fixed a lot of cars and was good at breaking them – breaking and fixing, a bit of both! And that's how I learnt, by watching him.

We didn't have much money. So that's why we had to buy the cheapest car. Dad would go to Darwin, get a car and then drive back. I stayed home and then weeks later, my dad would rock up with a car.'

I asked Chico what they used the cars for.

'To go to the bank, clinic, shop – and hunting. For hunting, it's easy in the car instead of walking.

If the land is rough, the car won't last long. For example, buffaloes and pigs walk on the land, they dig out the plants. And that's what makes it hard for us to get out on the Country and hard for the car to survive.

In a way, you have to make your own road to get to places.'

Jerome and Chico salvage car parts from the dump, Ramingining, Northern Territory.

'So what do you do if something goes wrong with your car?' I asked him.

'Nowadays, if you go to the dump, you get a lot of free parts.

If I got a car here and then drive back, there's a lot of cars similar with the same parts.

I make things work. For example, if I go way out in the bush, out in the flood plains, and something goes wrong, I think out of the box. I make the car go.'

'What if your car has no brakes? Is that the end of the car?'

'If you have a manual, the gears help with the braking. You shift the gears from five down to one. And then from one, then you go to reverse, then stop the car.

Clutch goes, you use the handbrakes, or you just run into an anthill or something.'

'Is it important for Yolngu to have a car?'

'It is important because you can go a lot of areas: hunting, camping, or if there's a funeral, you can go there with the vehicle. Before that, people used to walk. Sleep, walk, sleep, walk.'

'What are your best bush-mechanic skills?' I asked Chico.

'Ooh, so with electronic, I'm not good. But with bearing or something that can break, it is fixable with wire and stuff, you know? Like with a bit of fencing wire I have fixed the steering rod or the steering arm. Just twist and twist and then you use pliers and twist and twist and twist and off you go.'

'And your favourite bush tucker?'

'Wallaby or kangaroo.

Everything we catch, we cut and cook the traditional way. I got taught by my father and my granny the skills of life, and culture, of course.'

The car that wouldn't die

Shooting a scene from *Black As* where the Hyundai pulls Suzi out of the mud hole.

After the Suzuki went to car heaven early in the making of *Black As*, we needed another car. As luck would have it, a mine worker at Gove, a few kilometres away, posted his unregistered Hyundai for sale for $200. At first it was, 'Hyundai?! Surely we can lay our hands on a Holden, Ford or Toyota!' How wrong we were!

We grabbed the Hyundai pronto and got it the few hundred kilometres to Ramo. It had to be *Black As*'d, so the boys took to it with axes and hammers and gave it a complete makeover. The Hyundai was then 'found' at a badly ravaged outstation, 20 kilometres from Ramo, and took on its new role as a 'go anywhere, do anything' car.

It turned out the poor little Hyundai was virtually indestructible. With seats missing and the windscreen gone, and half-hacked to death, it just kept going. Its most remarkable feat was pulling the beloved Suzuki out of knee-deep mud then towing it to its fiery grave.

Long after I went home, the Hyundai lived on as a hunting car. The boys would send me photos and videos of their hunting expeditions, the little blue rocket packed with friends and family and adorned with bleeding kangaroos, limp mangrove geese or shimmering barramundi. They were proud of their hunting prowess and the tenacity of the little Hyundai.

But the churned-up buffalo playgrounds were eventually too much for the Korean warrior and it was given a rest out the front of Chico's house. Apart from its ravaged body, all it needed was a new clutch, motor, suspension, wheels and a mechanic god to descend from the heavens to breathe life back into it. Unaware of its iconic status (or jealous of it), Ramingining Council towed it to the dump to join all the other deceased vehicles that had been flogged to death. When we returned to shoot season two of *Black As*, the boys made a return visit to pay respects to the Hyundai. Sadly, it had been piled up with the carcases of dozens of other tortured modacars then set on fire by unknowns who gain pleasure from the smell and toxic fumes of burning cars.

Joe

Joseph was born in Cootamundra in New South Wales and is of European extraction, but he went to school and grew up mostly in Ramingining. His bush skills and ability to problem-solve are remarkable. He has been through full Yolngu initiation and speaks the local Djambarrpuyngu language fluently.

Joe speaks: 'My father found a new job working at the Resource Centre and my mum worked at the shop that was on the side of it. And then I was going to school at Ramingining. In school I was picked on a lot. I was the only white kid in the school at the time. Because I hadn't been to Ceremony; I hadn't been initiated. They would call me Pink One, all these names. Just the normal teasing that you get day to day.

'My parents spent two to three years in Ramo and then they left town. I decided to stay on, but dropped out of school. I was 15.

I stayed with my local Yolngu family. They were my neighbours growing up. Trevor and Jennifer and two sons, Jethro and Franco, my brothers. I was hanging around with another group of boys that were getting into mischief. Then Trevor and Jennifer spoke to me and said: "You've got to stop getting into mischief." And then they started disciplining me and took me under their roof. I got a job at Murwangi Cattle Station, about 35 kilometres from Ramingining, the old Arafura ruins. But it's not operating anymore.

'I decided to [go through law], and the Elders said okay. It was a process. And here I am today, respected by the boys and the community. I was about 17. A lot's involved, a lot of organising. It's a system that's in place, and people know what's going on and what's to be done. It's been in place for a long ... long, long time, and it doesn't change. Like, in the white world, everything's always changing: laws are changing, parliament's changing. In the Yolngu law, it doesn't change. And yeah, I was selected to do what most Yolngu men do in Ramingining.

'We go into the bush and then you're not allowed out, depending on how long the ceremony goes for. Sometimes it can be up to six months to a year. You stay in one place in the bush, live off the land, get taught by the Elders, discipline. You're recognised as a man and you've got responsibility not to be silly or stupid or touching people's belongings, things like that: handbags, cars, not allowed to steal.'

I asked Joe about his first car. 'It was a Mini Moke we bought off the shop manager. My Yolngu brother and I bought it from ice-cup money; we used to sell ice cups. I was 14. No licence, no registration, no rules. We were down at the creek, and I thought I'd reverse it into the water a little bit to wash it. But I didn't realise how light the Mini Moke was. So, I reversed it, and it started floating away. Then I got flogged because the engine went under as well. And back in the day, the starter motors were really big and we could not get another starter motor for it. So we push-started it here and there, but then it died. Then I got a petrol ute.

'I met the boys on the outstation. I was married to one of their sisters. We used to have motorbikes, boats, and just loved being out on Country, being in the bush. I can't think of any other life to live. I still live that life to this day.'

'Are cars important for Yolngu these days?' I asked him.

'Yes, very important, because getting across Country isn't as easy as it used to be, with wild buffalo, wild pigs, wild cow. So cars are a lot easier to get from A to B ... I like problem-solving in the bush. There's always a way of getting something done. If you can't do it one way, there's another way to do it. If I need to get somewhere in the bush ... if you can't get across the river, you go around the river, even though it's longer. I like getting things done.'

'So why did you want to make *Black As* in the first place? Because the idea came from you guys.'

'I wanted to show the world how it is in the bush and how a non-Indigenous fellow can get along with Yolngu people. It doesn't matter the colour of our skin. If we put our brains together and want to get something done, we can do it. And we've got a culture that exists and a way of life in the bush that not many people get to see. And me and the boys, it shows how we pull together and we're all on the same page and having fun about it as well as frustrating times. But it's how we are.'

The Toyota HiLux two-wheel drive – destroyed, survived and lives again

Shooting season three of *Black As* was about as disastrous as it gets: we drowned the camera in sea water, were given unlivable accommodation, there was no production vehicle, no crew – the tale of woe is longer than a wet weekend. Except for one thing: Blacksy, the two-wheel drive HiLux that was donated to the boys to make another season.

Still in East Arnhem Land, this time around we were based in Gove and shooting in and around Yirrkala. Blacksy was thrashed harder than a Sydney Cove convict. Towing a boat twice its size uphill, half drowned in sea water, it just kept going. It was such a mighty beast that when we finished filming, Jerome claimed it as his, and drove it home to Ramingining, a corrugated and potholed 14-hour nightmare.

Now back on his home turf with a car, Jerome was as popular as a meat pie at the footy. Most days his family would pile in, over and on the top of Blacksy to go hunting. In photos of the expeditions, Blacksy was in its prime and loving it; it was, after all, an indestructible HiLux. Each night Blacksy would be parked out the front of Jerome's house at his outstation. First a wheel was 'borrowed' then two more wheels and some brake shoes, then it fell off the bricks that were keeping it off the ground, till poor old loyal Blacksy was given up for dead and was staring down the steering column of being relocated to the local dump and torched.

With season four of *Black As* in the pipeline, I was onto Jerome and Chico to look after Blacksy's welfare and stop any more part-thieving. Above all, they had to stand in the way of any attempts to tow it to the modacar graveyard.

A few months later, we arrived back in Ramingining. Our number-one objective was to get Blacksy to rehab and back on the small screen. I knew all the wheels and brakes were missing. No brakes the boys could handle, but the prospect of finding wheels with tyres or carving them out of wood was as remote as Ramingining itself. I managed to pick up some second-hand rims and tyres in Katherine, and arrived in Ramo, tracked down Blacksy and went about pimping the ride with Chico, Dino and Jerome (Joe was busy pouring concrete).

Unfortunately, the wreckers in Katherine sold me the wrong rims, so we had to cut the centres out with an angle grinder to make them fit onto the wheel studs. With no brake drums, we simply put a few on washers to make up the gap. But it was the tie rod end that posed the biggest threat to Blacksy's return to fame: it had fallen prey to the evil part-snatchers, making the Black Princess unsteerable.

Luck plays a central role in all remote bush-mechanic TV productions. Ingenuity comes a close second, and bulging muscles are another must. Chico knew of another identical HiLux at the dump with all the steering rods and knuckles intact, so we trotted off to locate it and remove the tie rod end.

Luck was with us: sure enough, the HiLux was there, perched high on top of five other doomed cars. Another factor in play while creating madcap TV shows involving cars and a bunch of lunatics in the middle of nowhere is near-death experiences. On this occasion, the person at the pointy end of this near-death experience was me. It occurred after a snatch strap was fastened to the spare-parts HiLux and the other to our Toyota troop carrier production vehicle. I was at the base of the car pile retrieving what looked like a perfectly good car jack when the driver of the pulling car dropped the clutch, slammed down the accelerator and yanked the trashed HiLux down off its perch in a trajectory aligned with my head.

Chico let out a yell that could break inch-thick glass: 'BATTY!!' Glancing up, I saw the donor car tumbling down towards me. With all my human and superhuman strength I sprang out of its way like a surprised cat, the HiLux tailgate clipping my leg hairs, catching my left thong and squashing it to the thickness of a cigarette paper. A small price to pay.

With the unscheduled dramatic element out of the way, Chico and Jerome went to work removing the tie rod end. Without the standard $20 device known as a ball-joint separator (any bush mechanic will tell you a ball joint doesn't separate easily), it requires a good 15 minutes of continuous smashing with a hammer or axe to get it apart. After much bashing and grunting we had ourselves a brand-new used rod of steel that would get Blacksy back on the road to glory.

Driving a car with zero brakes is not for your average suburban driver – or any driver for that matter. It's specialist knowledge that has been handed down through the generations in remote Aboriginal Australia and coveted as a badge of honour by the novice driver yet to earn their stripes behind a steering wheel. The technique goes like this: when you want to bring the chariot to a standstill or just slow down to walking pace, the car is slipped into reverse gear and the clutch gently and slowly released. The modacar is tricked into thinking it's time to go backwards but has to slow down to do it. This age-old technique was employed the entire time through the shooting of season four, when the beloved Blacksy was hacked to pieces by baddies, squashed under the load of a huge dinghy, bulldozed through thick scrub, sent after buffalo, and had the radiator speared and grease used as engine oil.

When filming was done, Blacksy loved nothing more than to hurtle over jumps, do a dozen doughnuts at a time, ram trees and, most impressively, perform long sideways drifts. This pastime was usually under the influence and rally-driving abilities of Joe. Blacksy just kept going, returning once again to its tranquil life as a hunting car. By all accounts it's still going strong.

Craig Rees and Dave Nixon securing swags, returning home from a *Black As* shoot, Tennant Creek, Northern Territory.

6

Me, Jen and Mikey en route to disaster! Ngumpan Cliffs, Great Northern Highway, Kimberley, Western Australia.

WHERE TO CAMP

After living in Broome for a few years, with a fair few of those years out bush, I thought I knew it all. So it was business as usual as I prepared to do a reccy for an ABC doco to be called *Rodeo Road*. Three of us – producer Jen, stills photographer Mikey and me as writer, director and cameraman – would be merrily heading to cattle country in the heart of the Kimberley. The twin-cab HiLux was packed with everything we'd need: swags, tuckerbox, billy box, a full water tank and some basic camera gear. We'd be hanging out with genuine Kimberley cowboys, station workers who, in their spare time, put their life on the line riding crazed bulls, bucking broncos and wild bush horses.

It was late April. The wet season had almost passed, taking the sticky humidity with it. But by mid-afternoon, the blue skies were turning dark. A hundred clicks out of Fitzroy Crossing, it started: the tail end of a cyclone that had already wreaked havoc around Port Headland was racing east into the desert to wreak more. It was like we'd driven into a waterfall lit by intense flashes of lightning that would rival the brightest disco strobe light imaginable. When you raised your hand you had instant X-ray vision and could see knuckles, joints and the bones in between.

Should we stop and see if it passed, or keep driving and try to get to the other side?

I put my foot to the floor.

Just out of Fitzroy Crossing, I managed to put the storm from hell behind us. We kept going to our first appointment with Louie Dolby, a larger-than-life Bunuba man who was running a few thousand head of cattle and a team of crack Aboriginal ringers at Mount Pierre Station.

Mikey netting for cherebin (freshwater prawn), Galeru Gorge, Kimberly, Western Australia.

I'd prearranged with Louie that we'd camp near his homestead at Galeru Gorge and catch up the next morning. So we drove down a steep bank through a shallow stream and set up camp by the gently flowing river that exits the majestic gorge.

After a swim in the cool dark waters, we rolled out the swags, threw a T-bone each on the coals and knocked back a few beers. How could you get better than this? Even the stars seemed to agree. We eventually dozed off in our swags, serenaded by the gentle sound of lapping water.

At around 4 am, I woke up with wet feet. I strapped on the headtorch and switched it on. The trickling brook we'd camped beside had turned brown and was pushing branches and debris along. I could see that it was rising – fast!

I began to shake, gripped by a combination of fear and panic. 'Fuck! Fuck! Fuck!'

Now Jen and Mikey were wide awake. With no time to roll swags or do anything in an orderly fashion, we threw the billy box, tuckerbox, swags and everything else onto the roof of the HiLux. Then, driven by the kind of adrenalin only impending death can trigger, we took on the now raging river in the dark.

Soon water was halfway up the doors. With no snorkel, we managed to reach the bank on the other side but it had turned into a steep, muddy slippery dip. I slammed the HiLux into low range and in first gear only *just* managed to reach higher ground.

Dawn light revealed the scene: a wide brown raging river, now 3 metres over the spot we'd been camping just minutes earlier.

The storm the day before had dumped its load tens of kilometres away, some of it in the catchment of Galeru Gorge. We'd only just escaped but we'd learnt our lesson big time: beware of camping in riverbeds! And beware the tail of a cyclone!

Don't be like us. After being behind the wheel for a few hundred kilometres or if you're just a road-weary passenger, you want to find somewhere to rest your head where you can be sure of waking up in the morning.

Home away from home at Flat Rock, Dampier Peninsula, Western Australia.

Powered-site dinosaurs

Gone are the days when a van owner's only option was to plug into a powered site to keep the butter firm and the milk from going off or, stuck on a cryptic crossword puzzle, at risk of draining the car battery under a nightlight. These days most vans and caravans and big tent set-ups have solar panels and a battery to store the sun juice. Powered sites are handy if you lack independent solar power or want to make a replica of your living and cooking arrangements at the hacienda back in suburbia. The flashier vans and campervans often come with built-in showers and even washing machines, so we don't need the van parks as much. Besides, these days, for most caravanners and campers, it's all about free camping.

Finding the perfect spot

So how do you find that perfect spot?

In daylight, is how. In fact, start looking for a camp way before the sun turns into a faint glow on the horizon. This will allow you to set up and get dinner on without the need to be fumbling around in the dark. Plus, you'll have time to kick back with a cold refreshment by a fire while you wait for the camp oven to deliver its scrumptious contents.

Some jurisdictions encourage free camping.

Some states, territories and jurisdictions actually encourage road warriors to pull up by a road and camp the night. They might even provide bins, toilets, barbecues, shade areas and toilet waste dumps. But what if you want to find a nice quiet spot away from everyone else, or you're in the middle of nowhere and just want to pull up away from the road?

There are a number of mobile apps that show you the locations of overnighting options, which can be super helpful. But if you want to find a nice quiet spot on your own – especially if you're swagging out like I do – here are a few tips.

Unfenced land

Fences are designed to keep animals in and you out. In remote areas, look on both sides of the road for unfenced land. Then any old track will usually take you away from the road to a quiet spot – and with any luck a clearing or cleared area big enough to park your home on wheels or swag out.

Abandoned quarries, airstrips or road camps

My favourite spots for free camping are abandoned quarries, airstrips or road camps, because they're usually large, flat and cleared making them perfect for retiring in the horizontal.

To find such a place, look for heavily used tracks that head off at right angles to the road. With any luck, such a track will lead to a relatively quiet area away from the bitumen and howling road trains.

Alternatively, if you're in mobile range, go to the map app on your phone and change the screen to satellite view. Search for open or cleared areas away from the road that have a visible access track.

Sometimes the tracks might have grown over or are not obvious from the road.

Such clearings are nearly always covered with gravel or the crushed rock they use to make road base. There might even be mounds of gravel or piled-up dirt to provide privacy and a windbreak. Here you will have no falling tree branches to kill you, you'll be flat and level, and there will be little chance of your campfire setting the scrub alight.

The downside is that these clearings are nearly always devoid of firewood, so you'll need to get some on the way in.

If you're swagging or tenting, keep well away from big, dark stained patches, as they could be diesel or chemical spills that will drive you nuts with the smell. This happened to me on a recent drive up the west coast of Western Australia. After a long day of driving, we were pushing into last light near Port Headland and desperate to make camp, cook dinner and crash. We turned down a recently used track to find a perfectly wide, flat cleared area. Without scouting our overnight digs, we hastily made camp. It turned out there was a diesel-soaked spot a few metres away that sent a toxic pong over our swags all night. It was like sleeping next to a leaking diesel bowser.

Roadside gravel pit camp, Kalbarri, Western Australia.

Transit camp by the Murrumbidgee River on crown land.

If it's the dry season, look near a creek or river

Check the map and search for a place where the road crosses a creek or river. There's often a track off to the side before the bridge or causeway that may take you to a supremo spot. This is only advisable in the dry season – flash floods are a real thing (as I have explained in lurid detail). If there's rain about or has been in the catchment, DO NOT CAMP IN A RIVERBED.

Making camp

If you're on a road-trip mission and free camping as much as you possibly can, it pays to have a comfortable, safe, overnight camp where you will get plenty of sleep.

Find flat ground

Flat ground makes for a roll-free sleep and keeps you on the level. If you have little choice, make sure you position your sleeping arrangements so your head is uphill.

Shooting a classic scene from episode one of the *Bush Mechanics* series. The band is trying to get to a gig in Willowra, Northern Territory, in the never-say-die Holden HJ. *Hugh Miller*

A drive to or from Alice Springs usually means stopping to grab lake salt when it's dry. My daughter Gina on Lake Hart, South Australia. *David Batty*

Jen McMahon and I were asked to create a replica of the Ngappa car as seen in episode four of *Bush Mechanics*. Francis Jupurrurla Kelly and Thomas Jungala Rice painted it at Yuendumu. It's now at the Australian Centre for the Moving Image, Federation Square, Melbourne, with a Mad Max car making up the other half. *Mark Natoli*

Travelling buddy Narelle at our seaside camp near Monkey Mia, Western Australia. *David Batty*

My son Chris and his HiLux were support for a convoy of troop carriers carrying Yulparija Elders to their birth places at Percival Lakes, Western Australia, to paint canvases. He deviated off the side of this lake and skidded as if it was ice. *Michael Hutchins*

The road to Tunnel Creek in the Kimberley cuts though the bizarre Devonian landscapes of the Napier and Oscar Ranges. *Narrelle Perroux*

Waking up in your swag to a London fog on the Nullarbor is just another day on a drive around Oz. *Narrelle Perroux*

The *Black As* boys 'borrow' Uncle Oppy's dinghy. Without a trailer, some bush ingenuity gets it onto poor old Blacksy the HiLux. *Jono Van Hest*

Oh no! The *Black As* boys manage to drown their beloved Suzuki. Towing it out a few weeks later with a Hyundai was next level retrieval. Ramingining, Northern Territory.
Jono Van Hest

Finding gems like this beachside camp on a one-week bushwalk was heaven-sent. We stayed two nights enjoying freshly caught fish and abalone. South coast, New South Wales.
David Batty

After days of bush bashing a tractor from a remote community to get it home to its owner …
it conks out! Joe and the postie bike come to the rescue. Ramingining, Northern Territory.
Jono Van Hest

We often go through Burra in South Australia to and from Alice Springs or Broome. My
daughter Gina and I found this top camping spot at a quarry nearby. *David Batty*

Walking and camping the south coast of New South Wales is hard to beat. Wake up in the morning and take a dip in paradise at Middle Beach. *David Batty*

Sometimes you just have to stop and take it all in. Exploring bush tracks in southern New South Wales. *David Batty*

Broome locals have their 'spots' where they know they will be able to hook a few muddies. We have ours. *David Batty*

After a long day behind the wheel from Katherine, Gina finds a perfect boab for a beer and breather before making camp. Near Kununurra, Western Australia. *David Batty*

Avoid deadly branches

It's written in stone going back to cave-dwelling Neanderthals that you don't camp under trees with overhanging limbs. I have friends who have been killed and others crippled for life from branches snapping off and dropping onto them. If you live among trees, you soon become aware just how many shed their limbs – and not just the lower ones. Another good reason to find a clear, flat area.

Look for or create a windbreak

If you're in a van or tent, the following may not apply, but you might pick up a few handy tips. I've spent countless nights in my swag by a fire under the stars, and a lot of those camps have been with this continent's original campers, the Indigenous folk who have been doing it for ever. They apply a simple logic around fire and swag placement that is now a hard and fast rule for me, my family and any of my camping mates. It's about wind. In desert areas my Aboriginal camping companions have often gone to great lengths to make a horseshoe windbreak from spinifex up to a metre high. They build up the spikey clumps like giant hairy Lego blocks, and some such windbreaks have accommodated a dozen people or so.

Most areas of Australia have a prevailing wind – the direction the wind predominantly comes from. In coastal areas the wind can swing around more but in the interior it's almost always from one direction in the evening, and that's often from the east.

The idea is to have the wind in front of you so when you lay out your swag your head end is where the wind is coming from. I usually travel with an oyster suitcase and at night I use it as a windbreak. But anything that slows down the wind above your head will work – billy box, tuckerbox, chairs. Just something to tuck your head against to cut out any chilly, annoying breeze. This also means you're upwind from the campfire smoke.

SPINIFEX

This spikey native grass grows in tussocks throughout Australia, except for Tasmania. It was once the dominant grass species throughout the arid regions, in particular in central Australia. Sadly, it is slowly being wiped out by the introduced and  highly flammable buffel grass, which occurs in Africa, India and Indonesia. Buffel is also responsible for the rapid loss of flora and fauna through vast regions of arid Australia.

Spinifex resin is used by many Aboriginal tribal groups for securing shards of rock on the tips of spears and other tools and weapons. It's made by smashing down large quantities of the grass and collecting the resin, then melting it on a fire to make a super-hard ball of resin. Spinifex resin is also handy for repairing radiators. The Warlpiri word for spinifex resin is palya, while in Pitjantjatjara it's known as kiti.

Get a fire going

Whether vanning it or laid out on a swag, we all love a campfire, and being outdoors is a lesser experience without one. That is, if you're permitted to have one, and there are no fire bans. Pick a spot for your flickering flame maker of joy, slightly downwind if possible, leaving enough room for chairs and swags, and a space to cook on.

The best wood to collect for a fire is a hardwood, such as eucalyptus or mulga. Gidgee is a type of wattle and considered by every bushy worth their woollen socks to be the best firewood going, but it's only available in some arid areas. Slim Dusty even paid tribute to it in his melancholic song 'By a Fire of Gidgee Coals'. If you're cooking on a campfire, gidgee coals are by far superior even to mulga. A golden rule is to leave well alone any hollow logs or timber that might be a habitat.

The practice of creating a fire ring out of stones is something I've never adhered to. To me, it's unnecessary and tends to become a permanent fixture rather than allowing things to return to how they were after a few weeks or months.

Leaving firewood for the next happy camper when you depart is a top camping practice and one to be applauded.

Unleash the camp oven

It's time to get the camp oven on the fire. Here's how to do it. If you need some inspo, check out a few of my go-to camp recipes at the back of this book.

Make a bed of hot coals

You'll first need to build a decent-sized campfire then let it settle down till you have a pile of red-hot coals. Then, with a shovel or stick, move most of the red-hot coals to a spot about 20 centimetres away from the fire. You can now rekindle the campfire, which I recommend you do, as you may need to replenish the bed of coals.

Put the camp oven on

Place your loaded camp oven on the bed of hot coals with the lid on. It's now ready to cook its delicious contents.

Check often

Things cook faster in a camp oven than a household oven, so check it often. A roast dinner usually takes about an hour.

Replenish the coals if you need to

You may need to lift the camp oven off the bed of coals and replenish the coals with some fresh ones.

This will depend on cooking time, how thick your bed of coals is and the type of firewood you used to make the fire.

Enjoy the rewards

Slide or lift the camp oven off the coals and leave it where it will still get some warmth from the fire to keep the leftovers warm for the greedy, the extra hungry or those who just need to eat more 'cause it tasted so damn nice.

Plating up

Being in the bush you don't have to worry about cracking, chipping or smashing to pieces your best crockery, because you have left that at home. Enamel plates are good but can chip and are hot to hold; the good ol' melamine is my go-to dinnerware.

Empty, wash and store the oven

When you have gone for your third serve and the tummy is well and truly satisfied, empty the camp oven of any remaining food and wash it with hot water only – no detergents! Then dry it and smear it with cooking oil before storing.

Talking to the flies

When nature comes knocking and you are nowhere near amenities like a flushing toilet, long drop or a composting arrangement, you'll need to take a shovel and walk downwind until you're a pong-free distance away from the camp. Then dig a small hole about ten centimetres deep and squat. It's always a good idea to bury the accompanying paper and leave no sign of the deposit.

If you're staying long-term in a bush location, it will be in yours and everyone else's interest to create a temple of poo by digging a hole at least half a metre deep and placing a shrine on top so you don't fall in midway while having your deepest thoughts. Seating shrines can be the collapsible variety from camping shops, or you can make your own.

You can shut out the roaming eyes of your fellow campers by hanging a curtain of hessian or cloth around a few steel pickets.

Quarry camp amidst the limestone monoliths in the Oscar Ranges, Kimberley, Western Australia.

CAMP STRANDED

Broome to Fitzroy Crossing, July 2023

Even the most well-planned and organised road trip can be punctuated by an unexpected halt to proceedings. This can be fun, present new opportunities or be a total pain in the rear end. But if you're out of danger, dry and well prepared with sleeping, eating and drinking arrangements, you can just bide your time, chill out and ponder the universe and all its wonders.

Cable Beach, Broome, Western Australia.

I was halfway around a lap of Oz with my road trip buddies Carol and Narelle and our three weeks in Broome was nearing an end. Being June and in the midst of the so-called dry season, the town was pumping with visitors and locals alike. We spent a week camped up at James Prices Point, an hour north of Broome, and checked out all the local beaches, my daughter's burlesque show, bands and trivia night at the pub, and made a mosaic on the floor of our host's outdoor shower in exchange for staying in her house for three weeks.

Just as we were planning our exit, a massive storm front swept in from the west and proceeded to dump biblical quantities of rain right across the continent, flooding the Kimberley, central Australia and, most dramatically, central and western Queensland. The unseasonal deluge cut off roads and highways in all directions and washed away the temporary roads across the Fitzroy River at Fitzroy Crossing. Only a few weeks prior, the mighty bridge there had been completely destroyed by record-breaking rain.

By all accounts, the Fitzroy would reduce back to its normal dry-season trickle and the makeshift single lane road would open in a day or two. Closed highway or not, our stay at our friend's had come to an end with the completion of the tile-and-pearl-shell mosaic. So we loaded up once again and hit the road to Darwin.

We were making for my good ol' quarry camp site 50 kilometres this side of Fitzroy Crossing, in the heart of the ancient Devonian Reef just off the Tunnel Creek road. It was Friday and we were assured the bridge that had washed away would be resurrected by Saturday, so it would just be an overnight camp at the quarry then we'd be on our way across the river.

About halfway to Fitzroy, bulging boab trees start to populate the open grasslands and the termite mounds were like sharp-peaked sandcastles. With the sun pinking the sky, we turned off the highway and made for my trusty quarry camp site in the midst of the Oscar Ranges.

The unique Oscar Range with boabs galore in Bunaba Country.

I've made this my go-to camp for more than 30 years. Set in the surreal Devonian landscape, with its limestone monoliths, caves, rock outcrops with holes going right through them and dotted with boabs, it has never failed to impress whoever I've brought here. The quarry and associated clearings cover a massive area. In the centre is a body of deep and crystal-clear fresh water a kilometre long. It was created by the extraction of limestone rock used to build the Curtin military base and airport near Derby, where long-time locals reported thousands of cement trucks pouring rivers of concrete into chambers under the ground, as well as building a full-sized airport capable of accommodating jumbo jets and all manner of military aircraft.

Once a limestone quarry, now a massive swimming hole, Oscar Range, Kimberley, Western Australia.

Watch Video: The Boab Story – where did they come from?

BOAB TREES

Often referred to as upside-down trees, boabs only occur in the Kimberley and the Victoria River region of Western Australia. They are an anomaly in Australia, being deciduous and totally different from all other native species. Some believe they survive from Gondwana times, when Australia was connected to Africa, where they also occur. But most experts believe they floated across the Indian Ocean either from Madagascar or islands in-between that have since been submerged.

Boab trees can hold hundreds of litres of water, but they cannot be tapped for drinking. The pith from the nut is not only edible but it tastes like lemon and is high in vitamin A and C. Aboriginal people from the Kimberley use a sharp knife to carve boab nuts with intricate designs.

Over the years the quarry camp site has served me well. We used it as a base camp for Circus Oz when I was camp captain for their Kimberley tour; it was dinner camp for our TV series Going Bush *with Cathy Freeman and Deborah Mailman; we've spent innumerable overnights with family there en route down south; and we'd camp there when we were shooting documentaries in the area. These documentaries were often related to Jandamarra, the Bunuba freedom fighter who led what some call the Bunuba Resistance Movement. Jandamarra held several groups of mounted police at bay for years, hiding out in caves and tunnels scattered throughout the heart of his Bunuba Country. He was eventually shot and killed in 1897, and his head removed and sent to England as a trophy.*

Watch Video: Jandamarra – Aboriginal Geronimo

Now we turned off Tunnel Creek Road towards the camp site. But instead of the usual one or two odd bods who happened to know this hidden gem, we were met with gypsy camps dotted throughout the scrub. When we drove up over the rise, we came across a circle of vans, wagons and tents that would rival a busy campervan park on the New South Wales south coast on Australia Day. Everyone was stranded and waiting for the Fitzroy River to go down so they could get back on the road to where they were going.

While I do like having my lesser-known camp spots all to myself, the vision in front us was like a pop-up music festival without the music. Around fifty happy campers had encircled a massive roaring campfire. There were mums and dads in camping chairs with beers. There were also hordes of children and teenagers, and with zero phone reception, there wasn't a screen in sight.

Intrigued and slightly intoxicated by the sudden change in ambience, we were like excited kids ourselves. The delicious aroma of curries and stews from the serious collection of camp ovens wafted our way.

We stopped and enquired whether there was any intel on the road opening.

'They reckon Sunday at the earliest. Come and join us if you like!'

We politely declined and made camp amidst the ancient monoliths and spinifex back over the hill. Looked like we'd be here for at least the next few days – but no one was complaining.

After a hearty chicken stir fry and a glass of red, we ventured back over the rise to the circle of stranded vansters. Lit by their significant fire, their vans, trucks and four-wheel drives looked like glistening gems as we walked in and joined the group.

On the road camaraderie, sharing yarns and a few beers. Oscar Range, Kimberley, Western Australia.

My fears of an awkward silence or being told to piss off soon evaporated when I met Bernie.

His Santa Claus beard and broad Aussie accent immediately put us at ease. He was of a similar vintage to me and wasted no time in launching into tales of his wild upbringing in the opal town of Coober Pedy, Broken Hill and anywhere else his roo-shooting father took them.

He then moved on to his rig – a bright-red ex-Victorian rural Land Rover fire truck he'd picked up for a song and which was his pride and joy.

This was the indefatigable power plant that pulled his home on wheels, a genuine 18-foot, four-wheel-drive JB van. As a swaggie, I had to declare my ignorance of JB vans, only to be told it was the King of Vans, Aussie-made from the ground up and as bulletproof as Donald Trump himself. To Bernie, the JB stood for Just Brilliant. He insisted I get the full tour the following day. He would even trim his 'verandas' if I wanted snaps. My quizzical look invited an explanation: 'My bushy eyebrows. I'll get the missus onto them.' With this we headed back to camp with a promise to return the next day.

In the morning I decided to spark up the drone. I'm not a huge fan of the annoying gizmos and have always had a professional drone expert to do the job on shows like *Black As*. But given the unique scenery and having a few days to kill, it seemed as good a time as any to pop off some spectacular footage. I attached the mobile to the controller, pressed a button with some kind of hieroglyphic symbol and the drone whirred into action. It was still on the ground, so I pressed another button and it zoomed vertically into the air at lightning speed. A glimpse down at the screen and the view was unbelievable. Our camp was a mere dot amidst a bizarre landscape of rising limestone domes, crevices and jagged hills that stretched as far as the drone could capture. Then the drone was caught by a sudden high-altitude gust of wind and blew away to the north, never to be seen again. I'd blown the drone – lucky it was a hundred-dollar cheapy.

Not to be disheartened, and still wanting an aerial view of our camp and its surrounds, I climbed up a razor-sharp dome nearby. The view was, as I predicted, strange and ancient. The valleys and troughs of grey limestone cracks and caves reminded me of photos of the ancient Cambodian temple complex of Angkor Wat. With boab trees and tufts of spinifex dotting the lower hills, the sight was breathtaking.

Limestone domes dominate the landscape in this unique bit of Australia, Oscar Range, Western Australia.

Then down below I spotted a four-wheel drive towing a trailer with two bright-pink portable toilets. It wound around the gypsy camps and passed ours before depositing the pink thrones in a little valley below. My immediate thought was the relevant shire council must have been concerned about the population explosion in the quarry and the threat of dysentery, cholera or the spread of white toilet paper (which was already happening).

Then a convoy of 20 hire cars and four-wheel drives towing trailers full of strange objects came into view. They pulled up near the pink dunnies and a colourful collection of people emerged. They seemed lost and confused. One or two looked important and strutted about like they weren't happy. A person with multi-coloured hair went into deep conversation with an exceedingly good-looking young woman and man. The young woman had hair that would make Jimi Hendrix's afro look like a crew cut.

I came down from my mountain and walked towards what was now a car park of hire cars. At the same time, my new mate, Bernie, rocked up on the end of a leash. He was being pulled along by his young Alsatian pup. His verandas were trimmed and ready for action.

'Who's this mob, Bernie?'

'Stan. They're filming a movie. They reckon they booked the place out and want us all to pack up and leave!'

He burst into spasms of laughter.

'Good luck with that,' he muttered after he'd calmed down. 'I'm not goin' nowhere.'

We both had a good chuckle as we watched the Stan-dinistas charge off into the distance armed with cameras, reflectors, trolleys, monitors and a troop of colourful crew. Big Hair and her companion were obviously the talent, as they had devotees shading them under golf umbrellas.

Spying on the film crew in the midst of shooting a futuristic TV series.

'Yeah. It's about the last 11 people on Earth,' Bernie said.

As a filmmaker, I totally got it: post-apocalyptic desperadoes with great hair, immaculately dressed, walking through a landscape that looked like a movie set from *Planet of the Apes*.

We decided to do Bernie's van and Landie tour.

Bernie invited us into his van and Barb brewed some coffee. Barb seemed delightful, and once the coffee was served she sat down with us and put her arm around Bernie's shoulder, smiling. She seemed to adore him.

Both retired, they'd hitched up later in life. They'd head north when the chilly winter arrived in their home town of Bridgetown in south-east Western Australia.

'What've you got here?' I asked, looking around the van.

'We've got hot-water systems running on gas and diesel heating' Bernie said. 'A double bed we've extended, a chemical toilet, aircon, and the TV that's 12 or 240 volts. We've got two solar panels on the roof – two 150s, so that's 300 watts. And I've got the little portable one, which runs all the equipment in the Land Rover when we're parked up. We've got the Waeco fridge, a 2.5-litre washing machine. It's fantastic.'

'I love it,' Barb said.

'Mate, we can't be any happier than we are,' Bernie said. 'You've seen a pig in shit? Well, we're more than pigs in shit.'

I asked them how much water they carried on board.

'Two of those 95-litre tanks are just for all the domestic stuff in here. They're all plastic with sheet metal to protect them. Another is filtered for drinking water. Then we've got one dedicated grey-water tank, which takes all your kitchen water. So four tanks all together. The grey water tank is never full. You empty it into a specific grey-water area when you're camping in the caravan park. But most places you'll be lucky enough to put your hose on and run it over to a tree or run it away from your caravan a little bit.'

They clearly loved their van, but Bernie's pride and joy was the Landie, which still had 'FIRE TRUCK' emblazoned on the front.

'It's a 2003 Land Rover TDI 130. Turbo diesel injection, five cylinders, five speed. Brilliant. Love it,' he said. 'When I first got it, it had done 502 kilometres. It's souped up a little bit in the computer because it's a Victorian CFA firefighting unit. And they had to carry the unit on the back, which was a 10,000-litre mop-up firefighting unit. I wouldn't have been able to afford it brand new.

Bernie and Barb love their van and fire truck almost as much as each other.

'Look, I'm a Land Rover enthusiast and I get so much shit put on me for it. But there are more old and new Land Rovers on the road in this country than anywhere else. That's because 95 per cent of Land Rovers are still going. The other five per cent are used for parts. The army still uses them. There must be something in them.'

Both Barb and Bernie could see themselves caravanning well into the future.

'For as long as I'm alive and capable of driving, I'll be caravanning, holidaying, camping – whatever you like to call it. People say to me, "Were you born in a tent?" And I say, "As a matter of fact, I was." My parents and I travelled in a dirty great big tent, in trucks, Land Rovers, homemade campers, you name it. As soon as I got the opportunity myself, I got back into it, because I love it. I enjoy it. I find nothing more peaceful than sitting back in your camp with nothing urgent you got to do.'

They'd already been on the road for four months and their desire now was to head north and explore, meet others and gain relief from the arthritic pain caused by a cold winter in their home town. They were in no hurry to get anywhere and liked nothing more than to just mosey along the highways, pull over in out-of-the-way places and enjoy each other's company. Bernie had the full and undying support of Barb, who was more of a reader, and who did the cooking and domestic duties. They had a certain magic between them that impressed me no end and reinforced my belief in humanity, the power of love and new beginnings.

We left Barb and Bernie to themselves and spent the rest of the day exploring caves, spying on the film crew and swimming in the voluminous hole in the ground with the other strandees. As per most evenings, I was cooking the evening meal on the tailgate just before the sun gave up for the day. Then, out of the blue, two fit young chaps ran right through our camp in the direction of the mighty dome we were camped beside. To our shock and awe they started to scale the face of the razor-sharp dome. We were certain we'd be calling the Flying Doctor before long. But by some divine intervention they reached the summit, faced the setting sun and prayed. We were stunned by their stupidity but super impressed they made it.

Exploring the wonderworld of caves and rock formations in the heart of Bunuba Country.

We thought the praying was to attract angels to see them back down in the dark, but they made it safely back to ground level. As they strolled past our camp, I told them there was a much easier way to get to the top of the dome.

They informed us they were from Switzerland: climbing mountains was in their DNA. I said jokingly that if I knew they were coming, I'd have had snow dropped on the top. This was met with blank stares and 'Oh, okay,' – my bad Aussie humour had obviously not penetrated their austere sensibilities.

Just when we hoped our tortured day as stranded victims of nature's fury might end with blissful fireside chatter as we lay about on our comfy swags we were suddenly put under the spotlight! Not the fame or stage type, but glaring beams that could burn your retinas to a crisp. A monster truck towing a monster van that made it seem like a lit-up road train had pulled up next to our camp.

A human dwarfed by his oversized rig climbed down from the cab and strolled over.

'G'day, mate. We just came from the other side.'

Still in a daze from the spotlight, I thought he meant some kind of purgatory, a dark, lawless land of grotesque headless figures like a Hieronymus Bosch painting. Until I realised he'd brought luminosity to guide us into an enlightened world of modernity.

Realising we were beset by brain fog and still regaining our lost vision, he clarified.

'The other side of the Fitzroy River … The single-lane levy is up and running. You can cross to the other side!'

Back on Planet Stranded we jointly shifted our mindset and realised we were free to go!

7

Going a little too far into crab hole country, Palm Springs, Dampier Peninsula.

WHAT IF SOMETHING GOES WRONG?

Once, when I was living in Broome, I got a call on my brick from my number-one cameraman, Pauly. He was 100 kilometres up the coast in deep trouble, so had walked a few kilometres to a deserted Aboriginal outstation. Miraculously it had a working phone. Pauly was at a spot I was familiar with, but bogged up to the floor. He needed help.

I grabbed all the recovery gear I could lay my hands on and headed off. The track there involves driving along beaches, hopping over sand dunes and traversing the edges of vast mudflats. In the middle of the biggest tidal mudflat is a freshwater spring marked by an oasis of tall palm trees. There was Pauly, in notorious crab-hole country, where parts of the mudflats become infested with crabs that turn the ground into honeycomb, making it a giant car-eating patch of quicksand.

Pauly and his mate had been there for two days, shovelling out around the HiLux, trying anything and everything, but the ute had sunk up to the door handles into the gluey mud and was being sucked deeper by the minute.

The nearest crab-free hard ground was a fair way from the sinking HiLux. I got as close as I could in my HiLux without going down myself, then joined three snatch straps and a length of steel cable together. Once I'd connected an end to each ute, I got a decent run-up and *yanked*. Time and time again, my HiLux bounced back, as if it was on a giant rubberband. The straps would break, the boys would keep digging and Pauly's HiLux would move forward about 10 centimetres.

At this point, Pauly's philosophical born-again mate was telling him it was time to give up; it was God's will that things had played out like this, and we needed to let nature take its course and send his HiLux to the crab world down below. This only fuelled Pauly's frenetic digging.

As the sun started to sink over the end of the clay pan, with a huge run-up and with Pauly's foot to the floor, we finally extracted the HiLux. Exhausted and covered in salty mud, we quietly made our way home to Broome. It's true what they say about crab-hole country.

So even experienced cameramen like Pauly, who has got himself into countless pickles and knows the country well, can be caught out. The key is to be ready for anything and to have a few tricks up your sleeve. Here are some of mine, plus a few of the bush fixes I've seen over the years, some of which should *only* be executed by qualified and experienced bush maniacs ... I mean mechanics.

Bogged! What now?

Bogged in sand down to floor, what now? Ningaloo Coast, Western Australia.

You've been impressing your partner or your kids in the backseat with your excellent four-wheel-drive abilities, dodging rocks and boulders as you navigate a sandy riverbed or take on a steep sandhill. Then suddenly you sink deep – now you're not going anywhere. You're already in four-wheel drive, hubs locked, diff locked, but the more you rev the engine, the deeper the churning wheels take you down into a car-consuming quagmire.

Here's how to get out.

Reduce the tyre pressure

Using your trusty standalone pressure gauge, or the one on your compressor, reduce the pressure on all tyres, first to 170 kPa (25 psi) then, if you're still not moving, try 140 kPa (20 psi), then go as low as 100 kPa (15 psi). The science behind this manoeuvre is to increase the amount of tyre tread coming into contact with the ground. Once you're safely on hard ground, reinflate the tyres with your air compressor.

Recovery boards

Recovery boards are solid plastic boards about a metre long and 40 centimetres wide that you'll spot strapped to the roof racks of travelling four-wheel drives everywhere. They work a treat. Dig one in under each bogged wheel and drive your marooned chariot up and onto harder ground. Most people swear by them and never go beach driving without them. But sometimes you've gone down so deep you're going to need another solution ...

The big pull

A winch is a very handy item to have bolted onto the front of your car. This will more than likely get you out, if there's a good anchor point to hitch onto. A snatch strap hooked onto an accompanying vehicle might be able to yank you to firm ground or at least pull your wheels out of the trenches they've made. A combo of winch and recovery boards is a top idea.

If none of the above are working and you're as stuck as Tarzan in quicksand, things take on a whole new time frame and become a test of endurance and strength. Chances are that if you've tried all of the above and it's a no-go, the floor of your dream machine is sitting on sand or gravel and your wheels are just spinning helplessly. You may be here for a while, so take a break with a cup of tea and tell the passengers to get out and amuse themselves in the shade of a nearby tree or relax by the pool with a gin and tonic. You're going to have to lift the metal monster up and off the sand.

Jack it up

High-lift or 'kanga' jacks do a good job but are unstable and super dangerous. They're best left to expert hardcorers. As there is now no room under your vehicle to fit a jack, you'll need to get creative. This is where the bottle jack might come in handy. Dig the jack down or gingerly lift from anywhere that's safe and won't slip. Lift the wheels one by one, high enough to fill the craters underneath with rocks, branches or whatever else you can find, so long as the floor of the car is off the ground. If you are carrying recovery boards, now is a good time to place them under or in front of the wheels.

TO REV OR NOT TO REV?

This is a fiery topic that has reduced otherwise calm and rational four-wheel drivers to screaming demons around the campfire. Some say it's best to slowly engage the bogged wheels without over-revving. The other camp says it's foot to the floor and spin those rubber disks to a smoking fury. For me, the jury's out – I've seen both work effectively.

If you're in the mud ...

... you're in a dirty world of pain. If you've sunk deep into wet slushy mud your options are limited, especially if it's also teeming with rain. In this hellish situation, your only solution is the winch or snatch strap. Alternatively, make camp or check into the nearest roadhouse accommodation and wait till things dry out.

Other vehicle problems

HOW THE BUSH MECHANICS DO IT

Living in remote and often inhospitable places is what the original owners do best; it's their home and their land. Before Europeans hit the scene, they pretty much had a handle on

Black As boys and a very tired Blacksy, the HiLux that just kept going ... until now.

things in terms of food, shelter and ceremonial life. Everything came from the bush or ocean and tools were made from stone, wood or shell.

When they eventually had cars to get around in, qualified mechanics to fix them were thin on the ground, and so was the cash to pay them. If stranded on a remote bush track facing a long walk home, they had no choice but to fix the car. Being bush-craft masters and innovators from way back, they used whatever tools and materials they had at hand and worked it out. They had to become bush mechanics and fix cars like only they could. Here's what you can learn from them.

WARNING

The following fixes are for the desperate, bushwise or bush mechanic curious. Some are so dangerous you may need to check your personal insurance policy.

Hole or crack in the radiator

You're in a car, tearing around the bush on the tail of a kangaroo for dinner, when steam starts pouring out from under the bonnet. Someone takes a look under the hood and sees that a stick has speared the radiator, which is now hissing steam like a cut snake. What to do?

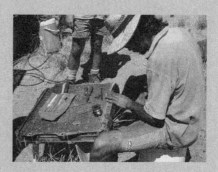

Well, someone gets a fire going while others hunt for a discarded dead car battery and an old frying pan, pot or hub cap. When the motor has cooled down, the radiator hoses are unclamped and the radiator is removed and drained. With the fire now a manageable bed of glowing coals, the hub cap or frying pan goes on the coals and the lead panels are placed in the cooking vessel and melted till silver and runny. Next, the part of the radiator that's cracked or leaking is also put on the fire and heated till red-hot. The radiator is then removed from the fire and the molten lead is poured onto the hole or crack and left to cool. The radiator is reinstalled and filled with water, and the hunters resume their dinnertime bush bash.

Broken fuel pump

Bush mechanics have several ingenious fixes for a broken fuel pump. I've seen a second fuel pump replumbed with long plastic tubing, which is then manually pumped by a passenger. Then there's the famous trick as seen in *Bush Mechanics*, where the windscreen-washer reservoir is filled with petrol and pumped into the carburettor by the driver activating the washer pump. But the tried-and-true, universal way to keep going is the old gravity-fed jerry-can-on-the-roof trick. Simply fill a jerry can or any other robust container with fuel from your tank and secure it upright on the roof of the vehicle. Disconnect your fuel line from the petrol pump and connect a metre or two of hose. Suck a bit of fuel through the hose to get it syphoning, then connect the hose to the carburettor line and you're away.

Broken spring

If you snap a leaf spring in your suspension by doing something ridiculous such as seriously overloading your wheels or taking on a few thousand kilometres of corrugations, all you need is a length of solid timber. Mulga is preferred, but  any hardwood timber about 6 centimetres in diameter will do. You'll also need some soft fencing wire, which you should always have on board.

Jack up the axle under the broken spring and remove the wheel. The length of wood should go slightly beyond the length of the spring. Using a Queensland hitch, wire the mulga around the leaf-spring shackles. Replace wheel and drive slowly to get a proper repair.

Broken wishbone

Wishbones are usually an integral part of the front suspension. Once broken, the car will slump down and be undrivable in a forward direction. This fix is only applicable to rear-drive vehicles and is advanced-level bush

mechanics only seen occasionally. First, loosen the wheel nuts and lift or jack up the broken front suspension and secure with fencing wire. Remove the wheel. Cut a metre-length of mulga or other suitable hardwood with a fork. Cut holes in the floor with an axe and wire the fork onto the underside of the vehicle, with the non-forked end facing towards the front. The forked piece of timber will now act as a skid instead of a rolling wheel, but will require the vehicle to be driven backwards.

Blown fuses

In older cars you could wrap the old glass fuse in cooking foil or the foil found in a cigarette packet to connect either end of the blown fuse. Fuses these days are little squares of plastic with flat metal forks. You can look into the plastic to see if it's blown or not. If it's blown, discard the plastic fuse and bridge the gap where the fuse was sitting with a little piece of wire. This works if you have figured out why the fuse blew in the first place. Otherwise with no fusing on that circuit, the wiring may catch on fire and the whole car go up in smoke.

Flat tyre

Remove the offending deflated tyre. Break the bead around the rim of the wheel and prise the tyre off one side of the rim. Stuff the empty space inside the tyre with grass, spinifex or clothing. Belt the tyre back on the rim, replace wheel and bingo ... off to do more dodgy motoring.

No engine oil

Your engine will still run if you top it up with water or pretty much any other liquid. Don't expect it to run for days or weeks, but it might be enough to get you to the car yard to buy another engine.

No brake fluid

Dishwashing liquid or washing powder will work as a brake-fluid substitute if you are absolutely desperate. But be careful not to use the brakes too much, as the soapy water will overheat and may blow your seals.

Noisy diff

It's an urban myth that bananas will quieten your noisy, worn-out diff. The *proven* method is to use sawdust. Even then, it'll only work for a short time, then you're back to a winding, annoying diff that will deteriorate faster and eventually seize up to the point you'll need a tilt tray to take your wheels to the nearest repair shop or metal recyclers.

Watery woes: when you run out of drinking water

There's nothing worse than running out of water. It's happened to me and it can happen to you. Whether it's a miscalculation, a leak in your container or an unexpected delay like being stranded or your car breaking down, it's something to be avoided. But if your tanks and bottles are empty and you've reached the dry-mouth, headaches and going-weak stage of dehydration, there are a few places you might find some water lurking. But beware: there are some totally useless techniques for finding water that will just make you thirstier.

Dig

If you can read the land like my Aboriginal companions have on various occasions, you can dig in the right spot to reveal a pool of groundwater. This might be in a dry creek bed, gully or low area. Sometimes the water will be quite shallow, or you might need to dig down a metre or so. Either way, once water is found, let it settle and go from dark brown to light brown, then drink it while being careful not to ingest too much leaf matter or gravel. If you're worried about bugs, boil it first.

Francis Jupurrurla Kelly drinks from an ancient rock hole, Central Australia.

Rock holes

These little rain-collecting vessels of nature occur throughout Australia. They have sustained our original Australians for thousands of years. Their significance and whereabouts are the stuff of song cycles and oral histories and are represented on many western desert–style 'dot paintings'. But more ephemeral rock holes and dish-like rock surfaces can hold rainwater for days and weeks – if it has rained! Even in coastal areas, fresh rainwater rock pools present perfectly good water to keep you alive.

My daughter Gina, immersed in mother nature, Jounama Creek, Talbingo, New South Wales.

Creeks and streams

Bush lore dictates that if it's flowing, it's okay to drink – but if it's still, boil it. Of course, that's if the watercourse originates from a pristine bush catchment. If it's flowing past a toxic waste dump or dairy, forget about it. Another gem of bush wisdom says a mile (yes, it's an ancient idea) of pristine creek, river or stream will clean its flowing gold into perfectly good drinkable water. I have drunk from nature's waters all my life without any known ill-effects, but in some places like New Zealand it's not recommended without boiling due to the giardia parasite, which can bring on a gush at the wrong end.

The *Black As* boys release a gush of drinking water from a melaleuca tree, Arnhem Land, Northern Territory.

Trees

To believe that boab trees hold drinkable water is to believe ice cubes grow on trees. But some trees *do* hold buckets of the stuff and are willing to release it if you simply cut into the trunk. I witnessed this amazing occurrence while filming an episode of *Black As* in Arnhem Land. We were shooting a scene where the boys were stranded and were lying on the ground apparently dying of thirst. One of the boys casually jumped up, grabbed an axe and started chopping into a nearby paperbark tree, also known as a melaleuca. Wherever he cut into the trunk the tree gushed streams of clear, tasty water.

Another theory is to find the right tree at the right location, dig to the correct depth, slice a root and fill your pannikin with tree-flavoured water. You will need a university degree in botany to distinguish which tree and its preferred location. Do not attempt if you're already thirsty or don't happen to have a shovel, crowbar, axe and cup handy.

For genuine tree-giving, life-sustaining and super-tasty refreshment, climb a coconut tree, toss down a green nut, slice off the top and guzzle.

The plastic-sheeting-over-a-hole trick

I have found this method of procuring the life-giving liquid completely useless. The theory is to dig a hole, place green leaves in the bottom and put a cup or bowl in the centre. Then place a sheet of plastic over the hole with a stone at the centre to draw a flood of microscopic droplets of condensation to the centre and into a waiting billy or pot below. Forget about it!

When you're desperate

If, through lack of water, you're about to wither like a prune and be mummified, there are a few liquids you can consume in small quantities without dying immediately.

- your own piss
- sea water
- animal (or human) blood
- windscreen-washing water (without additive)

Like most things between birth and death, anything can happen at any time. To allow for this often annoying accompaniment to life, especially if you're going into the wilds on wheels, it's a good thing to be prepared ... for anything. Think it through: will I be driving on sand? Is it so isolated I won't see another car for a week? Will it snow? What if a giant sun spot wipes out Eftpos! Don't leave home without it ... whatever that is!

THE TANAMI TRACK TIMING-BELT EPISODE

Halls Creek, Yiyili, Tanami Desert, January 1993

The Tanami Track is a 1100-kilometre mainly dirt road 'experience' that connects Alice Springs to the Kimberley at Halls Creek. It's a journey I've been taking since the late seventies. I lived in Alice for 13 years then Broome for another 12 and traversed the track countless times, so you might think that by now it would be like a drive to the front gate for me – but it's far from it. I've blown up motors, churned through mud for 50 kilometres, been witness to attempted murder, run out of fuel, performed epic bush-mechanic fixes, towed vehicles along its entire length, smashed windscreens and torn several tyres to shreds. But one of my most memorable Tanami episodes was when I was broken down and stranded for three days.

To tell this true and gripping tale requires some background info. In the early 1990s, word had spread of the *Sesame Street*-type children's films I'd made in Yuendumu, an Aboriginal community 350 kilometres to the west of Alice Springs. *Manyu Wana* or 'Just for Fun' was a ten-part numeracy and literacy series in the Warlpiri language designed to counter the flood of mainstream TV that was about to be streamed right across Australia and the Pacific via a new satellite service called AUSSAT. This new service would be available to anyone with a small satellite dish or who was tuned into a community-owned dish with a local transmitter. Warlpiri Elders and teachers were worried the new satellite would have a negative impact on local language and culture, and believed that locally made content in their language was a way to culturally guard against it.

A small independent school at a place called Yiyili, a few hundred clicks west of Halls Creek in the Kimberley, had similar concerns, and wanted the same style of children's films in their local language, Gooniyandi. The school sits on the Aboriginal owned-and-run cattle station Louisa Downs. So, I drove up the Tanami and set up camp by the Mary River on the edge of the community for a couple of months.

If you're living on a station in the Kimberley, it's impossible to ignore the dominant cattle culture and associated rodeo scene. To add some local flavour and content to the TV show, we decided to film the Halls Creek rodeo with Gooniyandi commentary. I was intrigued by, then totally hooked on, the colourful Kimberley rodeo scene. Virtually every Kimberley town from Broome to Wyndham hosts at least one rodeo a year.

They attract large crowds, who watch the local ringers, stock workers and enthusiasts risk life and limb riding on the backs of wild horses, steers and raging bulls. With ambulances at the ready, it's a nail-biting spectacle as the crowd cheers on a family member or fellow worker. It's also a time to catch up with other station workers and families, and there's evening entertainment and partying till all hours. It's a unifying force of black and white, and a fabulous display of horsemanship and skill.

After a two-month stint camped on the Mary River near the Yiyili school, all the filming for the kids' show was in the can. I packed my swag, camping gear and filming equipment, and headed off back home down the Tanami Track to Alice Springs.

A few months later, another rodeo in Halls Creek was announced. I managed to talk my mate Bill Davis into coming along for the ride. So, come January, we packed up my trusty old Toyota HiLux and headed back up the Tanami to Halls Creek to get among the rodeo long weekend. It did not disappoint.

Once again courageous cowboys and the odd cowgirl strapped on their leather chaps, lowered themselves into a chute and landed on the backs of frenzied horses and bulls. The chute door would fling open, releasing the animal, which tried as hard as it could to buck off or destroy the annoying human on its back. It's zero to hero for at least eight seconds of jolting gelignite to be in the running for a prestigious silver belt buckle and the admiration of the bejewelled but equally talented cowgirls.

Watch Video: Kimberley Rodeo Riders

Aboriginal stockmen with their badges of honour ... the gold belt buckle.

I became part of the day's entertainment, jumping into the ring with my TV camera to get as close to the action as possible without being killed. I'd run off videos of the day's events and sell them to cover fuel, hotel, tucker and a few hundred litres of brown fizz.

The Ringers' Ball was on the Saturday night, straight after the rough stock events, where the belt buckles were awarded. Around midday Sunday we hit the road and headed back down the Tanami towards Alice.

A few hundred kilometres down the track we stopped to relieve our beer-enriched bladders. I'd left the engine running and, on returning, the motor made a telltale metal-on-metal clunk. A puff of smoke rose from under the bonnet, then, after a short death rattle, the HiLux died.

My heart sank as I looked over at Bill. Our bulletproof cheerfulness evaporated, leaving a grim *oh no!* eyebrow-raising look of inevitability. We both knew this could be serious.

I slowly and gingerly wrapped my thumb and forefinger around the ignition key and gave the starter motor a touch. The resulting clunk went straight to my stomach and ignited not the motor but an overwhelming feeling of impending doom and the combined exclamation of 'Fuck!'

Desolate broken-down camp on the Tanami.

Bill and I stared off down the road to collect our thoughts. We let the realisation sink in that we were stuck ... badly. At that time of year, nobody in their right mind goes down the Tanami. A storm can make it impassable for days, and the nearest help was a few hundred kilometres away at Halls Creek. If a car did come by, then what? On top of this, the spot the HiLux had chosen to go on strike was a barren moonscape. The area had just been torched by a bushfire, leaving a black, charred landscape devoid of trees for shade or firewood. On top of this, a gnarly hot wind was swirling about, kicking up dust and fine sand. Bugger!

The old HiLux was a salvage job that had defeated the best bush-mechanic brains in a remote Aboriginal community in South Australia. I'd scrounged parts from the dump, and pieced the panels and chassis back together with a few welding rods, prayers and a dodgy wiring job. The electrics were a concept from its previous life as a hunting car for the community council office workers. Thus, no warning lights – and, more importantly, no timing-belt warning light.

Any prospective buyer of an old HiLux will know the importance of the intel around the timing belt. The belt has teeth and connects the crankshaft at the bottom of the motor to the camshaft at the top. It keeps the valves in sync with the rest of the motor. One tooth out, and you're in trouble. I'd got back on the Tanami in timing-belt ignorance, going by the old adage 'she'll be right' as my guiding principle. I wasn't a hundred per cent sure it was the belt, but with the motor not turning over, it seemed the most logical thing.

Bill takes shelter to make a Flying Doctor radio call.

We had a few things in our favour: a half-full 100-litre water tank, a few old label-less cans of food in the tuckerbox and swags. Being the era before mobile or satellite phones, the only way to communicate long distance apart from by smoke signal was radio. Luckily, I always carried my little green tin containing a lifesaving, never-fail gizmo: the Flying Doctor radio. With this you could make a three-minute telephone call anywhere in the world via the nearest Flying Doctor base, between 9 am and 5 pm, Monday to Friday. For us, the nearest base was Alice Springs, close on 1000 kilometres to the south. Being Sunday and a weekend, we had to wait till the morning.

We made camp on the edge of the road with a swag tarp tied to the side of the HiLux for shade. I was totally convinced it was the timing belt and wasted no time in removing the radiator and

Me and Bill wondering what the hell to do!

water pump to get to it. Sure enough, it was splintered into thin strips of rubber. There was nothing else we could do but resign ourselves to the predicament at hand and wait till we could make a radio telephone call in the morning when the Flying Doctor mob cracked back onto the airwaves.

As evening approached, the angry god of retribution turned the sand blaster down from extreme to high. The sun started to sink into a dull red orb and the temperature eased from a pizza-oven 45 degrees to a mild 30. The lack of firewood added an extra blanket of gloom: we were in for a night of total darkness. Apart from cooking food or boiling the billy, a fire delivers comfort and establishes a presence, like having the radio or TV emitting useless information in the corner of the living room.

Our half-dozen tins of anonymous contents were our only source of nutrition and comfort. We decided on one tin each and to save the rest in case our 'outdoor experience' booking was extended a further week – or even longer – by the invisible staff at Camp Corrugation. Our starvation-avoidance fallback position was to tuck into a box of Gravox powder, then dried French onion soup, and, as our last supper, we would share a jar of Promite.

We gingerly picked out a can each and opened them. My lucky-dip dinner was a can of processed peas, but Bill hit the jackpot with an all-time tuckerbox favourite, banana rice cream.

The gold was yet to be discovered, as I was certain there was a can of two fruits, a sugary stewed-peaches-and-pears mix with, if you were lucky, a cherry thrown in.

It was an early, fireless and particularly subdued retirement to the swags and a long night before morning tea arrived without the tea.

The Flying Doctor radio was a lifesaving marvel. It always worked and cost only $30 a year for a licence. For those living in remote locations, it was the only way of contacting the outside world, and it allowed people to tap into the telephone network and call anywhere in Australia.

All I had to do was lift the bonnet, connect the alligator clips to the car battery and throw the 5-metre antenna wire over the nearest tree – or, on this occasion, over the roof of the HiLux.

Just before nine o'clock I tuned the radio into the VJD (Victor Juliet Delta) Alice Springs Base frequency, then manipulated the dials until the little lights glowed most strongly. Then I waited for the Flying Doctor operator to finish their Iced VoVo and turn on their transmitter. At 9 am, the national anthem crackled through the little grilled speaker, demanding we stand to attention, face Canberra, place our hands on our hearts and rejoice in being young and free and stuck in the middle of nowhere.

With our patriotic duties attended to, the operator asked if there were any medical emergencies. It appeared there were no urgent medical calls, so after a brief, wavering silence she declared: 'Royal Flying Doctor Alice Springs VJD now open for radio telephone calls.'

This triggered a barrage of squeaky musketeers from distant desert locations yelling their call sign into their handpiece to get in the queue to make a call. Mine was Nine Delta Echo Sierra.

The operator wrote down each caller, read out the list so we knew our spot in the calling queue, and reminded everyone there was to be no bad language and that you only had three minutes. Then we had to wait our turn while listening to all the other callers' one-way conversations, with every sentence ending in 'over' so the other person knew when to talk.

Sandblasted, hot and hungry waiting for a new timing belt.

Perched on my bull bar, in blistering heat in a perpetual dust storm, I waited patiently for my turn. It was torture having to listen to each person's three minutes, which seemed more like half an hour. Shops ordered their monthly food deliveries – quantities of pies, frozen bread, fresh fruit and veggies; a school principal checked on the whereabouts of a student; someone enquired about the availability of accommodation; husbands called wives; on it went; 'Nine Delta Echo Sierra, go ahead, over.'

My first call was to the mechanics and trucking company in Halls Creek. Calls made on the Flying Doctor radio always seemed to carry a level of urgency that meant people on the other end of the line acted without hesitation. But after about two minutes of back-and-forth conversation punctuated with lots of 'overs', it became clear that it was going to cost a fortune for the mechanic and his offsider to travel 300 kilometres in a truck, do the repair and travel back. It was an exorbitant hourly rate for two, plus the parts and truck mileage per kilometre. The expense outweighed what the HiLux was worth by about ten times.

I got back in the queue and, after listening to a series of three-minute soap operas, whingeing teenagers and well-meaning rellies checking on Uncle Bobby in hospital, I was back on and talking to the Toyota spare-parts people in Kununurra, 600 kilometres to the north. Unlike the Halls Creek mechanics, they couldn't have been more helpful. Through the 'overs' I managed to convey my dilemma and get them to photocopy the bit from the HiLux manual that shows how to replace the timing belt and for them to get one on the nightly bus to the Halls Creek Trading Post. They didn't even ask for money, but I sent a cheque later.

Frank and One Mile in the Yiyili school Toyota.

My next call was to the school in Yiyili, asking if the school's workers, Frank and One Mile, could go to the Halls Creek Trading Post first thing to collect my belt and instructions, and then drive a few hundred kilometres down to us. Frank and One Mile were more than happy to do it.

Everything was now lined up so that, as soon as Frank and One Mile rocked up with the belt, we could get back on the road and home to Alice. All I had to do was install the belt and get the timing right, which was the nerve-wracking part. But for now, we had to wait it out on the side of a dirt road, cowering in a sandstorm in heat that would melt steel, while looking forward to dry Gravox powder for dinner.

People pay triple-digit sums of hard-earned cash and chew up their precious annual leave to languish about in exotic places, soaking up the sun and relaxing with a good book or nodding off while waiting to be served a freshly made caesar salad, all washed down with an icy-cold chardy. None of this was happening for Bill and me. We didn't even have a pack of cards or anything to read. Our stories were in for their third and fourth retelling, and we looked like burnt chops that had been rolled in red dirt. Forget henna: our hair was an organic shade of dust and our ears and nostrils required constant sand excavation.

Fireless, foodless and yarned out, all we could do was lie on our swags and wait till everything came into play in the morning. What could possibly go wrong?

The morning blew us out of our swags with a fresh dusting of red sand. Breakfast was not on the agenda.

A few hours on and anticipation was on the rise. I knew Frank and One Mile would have headed off before sunrise, and the bus would have dropped off the belt at the Halls Creek Trading Post when it passed through at 5 am that morning.

But come midday, nothing. I got back on the radio and called the Trading Post.

'Yeah, mate, the bus dropped it off on its way through this morning. Ah ... over?'

'You know Frank and One Mile from Yiyili? Over.'

'Yeah, mate. They my cousin. Over.'

'Any sign of them today? Over.'

'Yeah, mate, they picked up a parcel, early part. Ah, over.'

'Did they say where they were going? Over.'

'Nah, mate, but they bought big mob ice cream and packet chips.'

'Thanks, mate. Nine Delta Echo Sierra to VJD Alice Springs, over and out.'

Dumbfounded and mystified, I had to resign myself to the fact there was nothing more I could do. Bill had been good humoured and fun company all along, but he was starting to get that 'What have you got me into, Batty?' look. I'd known Bill for many years and he'd weathered many a drama, but he needed to get back to work and his family in Alice. Things were not looking good.

Then there was movement off in the distance, in the first sign of mechanical or even animal life in two days. I could see a cumulous billow from a vehicle approaching from the direction of Halls Creek. At last, the timing belt.

As the cloud approached, a white speck became visible beneath it. It looked a bit bigger than the Yiyili School Toyota, but we held our dusty breaths in anticipation. Soon a road train took shape and was bearing down on us. We decided to flag it down just in case it was carrying our timing belt.

Passing road trains just add to the fun.

A Tanami Transport double-decker triple-trailer road train, chockers with cattle and hurtling down a river of dust, is something to behold, especially when the brakes are applied in an effort to bring it to a stop. As if our current living situation wasn't dusty enough, the road train and its accompanying atomic bomb of dirt and the *cushhh, cushhh ka cushhhhhhh* of the airbrakes immersed us in dust as thick as a Pommy fog and with enough sand to rival the Sahara.

A decade later the dust settled, and a truck cab became visible along with a brown cloud of nose-biting cattle excrement. Finally a human wound the driver's side window. Bill and I coughed our way to the cab.

The driver seemed bemused by this vision of despair.

'Broken down, eh?'

'Yeah, mate, blew the bloody timing belt.'

'Faaaark. So, you're pretty rooted then?'

'Yeah. We got a belt coming down from Kununurra. S'posed to be here by now ... You seen a white Toyota along the way?'

'Nah, mate, can't help ya. Wanna beer?'

Our enthusiasm was enough for a cold beer to be produced from the oversized chariot.

'Can only spare one – keepin' a few more to get me to Alice. But I got a sticky you can 'ave.'

Being naive gentlemen of a refined persuasion, we were not acquainted with a sticky, but nodded in anticipation of something to eat. The road-train driver reached into his cab, retrieved something and tossed it down to us. It was a soft-porn magazine.

'Cheers, mate ... Thanks heaps.'

'No worries, boys. Not much more I can do. You'll be right.'

'Thanks, mate.'

The driver wound up his window and shuffled the gears, and the monster slowly lurched off in a cloud of bovine stench, leaving odorous pools of cow poo and wee right next to our enforced digs. Things *had* to improve, and soon.

The solitary can of beer evaporated down our collective gullets quicker than a bull out of a rodeo gate, just as we had seen days before. Then we kicked back and admired the photographic expertise and the physiques of the nude ladies in the sticky, and took turns reading the accompanying prose, which in turn gave rise to our enthusiasm to get home and get back on the nest.

An hour later a shockie-less Holden sedan bursting with human cargo came bouncing down the road from the direction of Halls Creek. I waved it down and approached the driver.

'G'day, mate. You come from Halls Creek?'

'Yeah.'

'See any broken-down car or Toyota?'

'Nah, nothing.'

'Thanks, mate.'

The whole thing was turning into a mystery bigger than the disappearance of Harold Holt!

The sun was nearing its final daytime destination. We picked out another two cans for another cold serving of mystery contents. Bill opened his first – spaghetti in cheese-and-tomato sauce. Then it was my turn. My belly was screaming out for a recharge of maybe Irish stew or the coveted two fruits.

As the can opener made its way around the lip it soon became obvious it was neither. Eventually sliced bamboo shoots were revealed. Whatever possessed me to buy them was as big a mystery as the disappeared timing belt. We decided to combine the contents of both cans and ate through gritted teeth, which is not easy.

At last light, a white Toyota ute loaded with women and kids came into view from the south. It looked like the Yiyili School Toyota but it couldn't be, because it was coming from the wrong direction. Halls Creek was to the north, and I didn't know of any crossroads.

Sure enough, the overloaded Toyota lurched to a stop. It was Frank and One Mile and a ute-load of mums and kids.

'Hey, Dave, we got your belt, mate. Got any tucker?'

As is the way with people around here, it turns out Frank and One Mile had no sense of urgency and did not share our anxiety to get the belt ASAP so we could get back on the road and back home. They saw the mission as a way of doing what they love most – going bush, and that meant hunting. Plus, they had a perfectly good Toyota fully fuelled up. The women were just as keen, and they loved to take the kids bush as well. There was a good chance of a fresh feed of kangaroo or goanna.

Frank and One Mile spent much of their younger years working on cattle stations all over the Kimberley and they knew every inch of it. I suspect One Mile got his name from being born on a station, possibly at a One Mile Creek or bore.

It didn't matter that they didn't have any food with them – I was just so grateful they came through with the goods.

'How come you came from that way?' I asked.

'We been hunting. The ladies were hungry for goanna and we been chasing kangaroo and bush turkey. But nothing. We went down that old station road that way.' One Mile gestured with protruding lips to the east. 'So no tucker, eh?'

'Sorry, One Mile, we only got one can left and don't know what it is.'

'You're right, mate. This mob full up from chips and ice cream anyway.'

By now it was way too dark to start on the motor and, besides, we hadn't packed any torches. We settled in for another fireless night. Our couriers slept on the ground without swags. First light they were up, back into the ute and off home to Yiyili. No fuss, no goodbyes, but clearly happy they'd had a day out hunting, even if they had no luck.

Bill's mood had lifted substantially. He's spent a lifetime living and working with Aboriginal people and he knows the Territory. He seemed impressed with my efforts to get the pages of the manual sent down with the belt.

Channelling all my inner bush mechanic to get out of this one!

Getting the timing right is absolutely critical, so I studied the pages of the manual, reading out the tech specs to Bill so we had two brains on it. I lined up the timing marks, slid the belt over the pulleys, then wove it around the tensioner. Then I went about putting the guards, hoses, water pump and the rest of the engine back together. My fear of failure was on the rise as we neared the critical moment of turning the key. I filled the radiator with a fair chunk of what water we had left following our visitors' departure. The time had come to test my standing as a fully-fledged bush mechanic. If I got the timing wrong, the valves could be out of whack and come down on a piston and put a hole in it – or even worse, bend the con rod, which would render the engine a complete write-off.

Before I turned the key that would shape our destiny, we decided to open the last mystery can from the tuckerbox. Bill ceremoniously handed me the can and opener. I pierced the top and levered the utensil around the lip and peeled it back.

Two fruits in syrup! A solitary red, glazed cherry bobbed to the surface. Yes! Our luck had turned.

With my heart pounding and catching worried looks from Bill, I hopped into the HiLux, wrapped thumb and forefinger around the key of fate and turned it. All the lights came on ready for action. I did a further turn to engage the solenoid, which would in turn kick the starter motor into action, which would in turn engage with the ring gear on the flywheel at the rear of the motor. Then I closed my eyes and gave the key the final little turn ...

Vrrooom! Dooka, dooka, dooka, dooka.

The old HiLux was back – and so were we, all the way home to Alice Springs.

Made it! Back over the border and home to Alice Springs.

8

ESSENTIAL DRIVES

Australia has its fair share of roads and tracks that cut their way through some of the most remote and inhospitable places on the planet. For well-equipped, super-organised and mad adventurers, there are the Birdsville Track, the Gunbarrel Highway, the Madigan Line, the Canning Stock Route, the French Line, the Binns Track and the Telegraph Track, just to name a few.

But for your average four-wheel driver who doesn't want to re-enact an Alby Mangels or Leyland Brothers movie, there are plenty of roads or 'highways' that offer spectacular scenery, adventure and places to explore without getting lost, breaking an axle or never being seen again.

All the roads described below require a rugged vehicle like a ute or a four-wheel drive. If you're towing a caravan, it will need to have been built for rough roads and have high clearance.

Daughter Gina, outback model, takes on the Tanami Track.

The Tanami Track

A billowing cloud of red dust delivers adventurous travellers from Alice Springs in the Centre along the Tanami Track to Halls Creek in the Kimberley, 1000 kilometres later. It weaves through a tapestry of mythological songlines and all too real stories of near death, extreme wealth and surviving in one of the most inhospitable places on earth. It looms large in my own family's jukebox of fireside yarns, and is the conception site and namesake of my first grandson – Tanami.

As I've mentioned, living in Alice for 12 years meant frequent trips along this long and dusty highway to Broome and the Kimberley. Consequently, I've had my fair share of breakdowns, heroic bush-mechanic fixes, blown-up motors and flat tyres. The Tanami cuts through the ancestral home of the Warlpiri people, some of whom had their first encounters with white folk looking for gold around the 1890s. My old Warlpiri mate Henry Cook told of the first time he saw white men near the original gold diggings at Tanami in the 1930s, with tragic and unexpected outcomes – but that's another story.

The journey is pretty well devoid of any mountains, rivers or epic views, but the overall sense that you are a lone voyager deep in the vastness of an unchanged land is humbling and exciting. If you are lucky enough to travel in the spring months, you're in for a floral feast. Tiny orchids, correa, all kinds of acacia (wattle) and blooming eucalypts are on show. My all-time favourite in beautiful abundance are the grevillea, especially the spider flower or honeysuckle, which can be sucked to release its clear sugary nectar.

Flocks of wild camels are a common sight as well as dingoes, perenties and, if you're super lucky and observant, a thorny devil lizard.

Beware corrugations.

History

Back in the day, reports of large deposits of gold attracted wealth-seeking men from the cities, many of whom fell victim to the unscrupulous sale of dodgy mining leases before perishing or retreating, penniless, to beer soaks in Alice Springs. In 1932, newspaper barons Keith Murdoch and Frank Packer sent journalist FE Baume along with a photographer to accompany geologist Cecil Madigan on an expedition from Alice Springs to the Tanami goldfields to report on the gold rush. Back then the route went through Coniston, the site of the last known massacre of our first Australians in 1928. Instead of finding a prosperous outpost glistening with gold, the journalist discovered starvation, death and desperation amongst men who had lost everything and had no way of returning to their previous lives. Baume returned and wrote a book called *Tragedy Track*. A few decades on, substantial deposits of gold were found that resulted in what today is a massive gold mining operation supporting 1200 fly-in fly-out workers. It's the second-largest underground gold mine in the country and to date has pumped out more than 10 million tonnes of the stuff.

The growing line of bitumen and when not to go

I drive the Tanami most years, sometimes a few times a year. The state of the 'track' varies according to the weather and how recently it's been maintained. For many years only the first 40 or 50 kilometres were sealed, then that was extended as far as the Aboriginal community of Yuendumu. On a recent drive, the track was in the midst of being sealed all the way to the Tanami gold mine, about 550 kilometres from Alice. The rest of the 450 kilometres to Halls Creek remains mostly unsealed.

After the track crosses the Western Australian border, it always seems to deteriorate.

Until the track is sealed all the way it's unwise to drive it in any kind of vehicle from at least December to March, unless you have first-hand intel as to its condition. Even then, proceed with caution.

Extra fuel is essential for doing the Tanami.

Filling up and the importance of jerries

If you want to go up to Halls Creek or down to Alice you'll need to carry fuel. You can buy fuel 24 hours a day at Tilmouth Well Roadhouse, which is 200 kilometres from Alice or another 100 kilometres up the road at Yuendumu. Theory has it you can also buy fuel at the Aboriginal community of Billiluna, about 150 kilometres south of Halls Creek, but I've been unsuccessful.

It's not advisable to rely on any of these options. The pumps may be closed or out of action or they may have run out of fuel. Not to mention the price! My advice and that of seasoned travellers and locals is to carry at least two 20-litre jerry cans and a funnel.

Linger no longer – Rabbit Flat

My own experience of the track goes back to 1976, when it was a rough-as-guts, two-rutted meander. When you crossed the border into Western Australia in the middle of nowhere it just got worse: chassis-bending potholes, shockie-killing corrugations and bulldust as deep as a Paul Robeson lament.

Halfway along the track was the 'remotest roadhouse in Australia', Rabbit Flat. Bruce Farrands lived there with his French wife, Jackie, and twin sons. Petrol was about as expensive as Tanami gold itself. It was sold via an ancient hand-pumped bowser that belonged in a museum. A large glass cylinder sitting high on the bowser was hand-cranked to the required number of gallons. In turn Bruce would kick a pebble to one side of the bowser to keep count of how many gallons he'd pumped up. Then a valve released the liquid and gravity fed it into your vehicle.

Bruce also sold grog, which was a bad idea and necessitated a corrugated-iron fortress around his home, bar and living arrangements. All transactions were through a square hole cut into steel mesh with a locking bolt that would keep out Genghis Khan with a wrecking ball.

Bruce and Jackie closed the road into their remote oasis in 2010, along with the roadhouse. Since then as I drive by I often wonder if they are still living in their galvanised-iron fortress or if they moved to the anonymity of a suburban home.

Typical off-road camp, mid Tanami Desert.

Making camp

These days we allow at least one overnight camp on the Tanami as it takes about a day and a half for normal people to get from Halls Creek to Alice. That range depends on breakdowns, making and packing up camp, topping up fuel from the jerries, lunch breaks and naps. There's any number of pull-overs, tracks, quarries and road work camps to roll out the swag or park your van.

There's Telstra phone reception at Tilmouth Well Roadhouse, Yuendumu and as you pass the Tanami gold mine. My preferred spot to make camp is a few kilometres north of the mine; it's in mobile coverage and I can check in with my loved ones.

The Gunbarrel Highway

In the mid-1950s the Gunbarrel was constructed by a team led by the legendary bushman, surveyor, artist and author Len Beadell. This 1350-kilometre stretch starts at Mulga Park Station near Uluru in Yankuntjatjara–Pitjantjatjara Country and heads due west into the depths of Western Australia. It was constructed mainly to assist in the monitoring of our first mainland atomic tests out of Emu Field and Maralinga and rocket tests out of Woomera in South Australia. It traverses the traditional lands of the Pitjantjatjara and Yankuntjatjara, and it cuts through Ngaanyatjarra and Pintubi Country as well.

Manning Gorge, one of many specky water holes along the Gibb.

The Gibb River Road

If you want to earn your stripes as a four-wheel-drive adventurer, 'the Gibb' is an absolute must. It's a 660-kilometre, mostly dirt road that runs between Derby and Wyndham at the top of the

Kimberley. It's the land of the Wororra, Wunambal Gaambera and Ngarinyin people, who still have strong ties to land the road traverses. Their rock art is widespread throughout this area, marking their long occupation and ownership.

Plan well ahead if you intend to add the Gibb to your itinerary, keeping in mind it's often closed between October and April due to flooding, when it's uncomfortably hot and humid anyway. Allow a few days, or up to a week to really enjoy everything it has on offer. Do your research or invest in one of the many guidebooks. Rules and regulations around camping change from year to year. A guidebook or online check will fill you in on all the camp spots, waterholes and accommodation options.

History

Back in 1880, applications were invited for pastoral leases in the northern Kimberley of more than 20 million hectares. The early pioneers and squatters with their sheep found the natural grasses too high in the wet season and of no use in the dry, and the sheep were soon replaced by beef cattle. Once it became clear that the squatters and their new animals intended to stay, conflict with the original owners of the land quickly emerged. In 1882 a settler was speared, which triggered 15 years of police retribution. The resulting Bunuba Resistance Movement led to a manhunt for Bunuba warrior Jandamarra, who was eventually killed by police.

As stations grew and grazing cattle became profitable, pastoralists constructed rough tracks linking stations in the west to Derby and Wyndham in the east. The tracks were hand hewn and just wide enough for bullock wagons and droving cattle. It could take over a week to travel with a supply wagon from Mount House to Derby.

In 1949, the government established the Beef Roads Programme and embarked on the construction of the Gibb River Road, which took three arduous years to complete. In the 1960s, explosives and heavy machinery helped cut a new direct route through the Napier and Wunaamin Miliwundi ranges. This opened up the western section of the track to beef trucks in 1963, but it took another four years to complete the works to make the Gibb River Road we know today.

Go early

If you want to travel on a road that's not chewed up by a zillion four-wheel-drives and caravans, with camp sites booked out or barras all caught, go early. In the north, mid-year school holidays and all of July see most of the travellers and campers, so May and June are the best months to go. If you're lucky, the corrugations may have been smoothed over by a fresh grading. There will be way less traffic and that means less dust, more parking at the popular spots and a better chance of a choice camp spot. Keep in mind that at peak season it's seriously busy. You may need to queue for access to a car park or camp site.

Take a plunge

The Gibb traverses the headwaters of the Kimberley's mightiest rivers, including the Isdell, Lennard and Fitzroy, and provides access to dozens of deep gorges and swimming holes. My all-time favourite is Bell Gorge, a peaceful, meandering watercourse lined with the ubiquitous pandanus and paperbarks. Crystal-clear water cascades down to a massive rock canyon ideal for swimming, then plunges down deep again to a pool best viewed from the top.

The gorge can be packed with fellow travellers, but there are plenty more rivers, canyons and waterholes to swim, camp near or catch a barramundi. Virtually all the waterways in this part of the world are inhabited by freshwater crocs. They are usually benign creatures and way smaller than their saltwater cousins. Wherever you swim you can assume they are there. Just leave them alone and they will leave you alone.

There are way too many camp and swimming spots to go into detail here so get yourself a map book or brochure, or download a map on your device.

Tunnel Creek, a must do in the heart of the Napier Range, Kimberley, Western Australia.

No need to go all the way

You can experience the best of what the Gibb has on offer without doing the whole thing. In fact, travelling west to east, I'd advise not going past the Barnett River Gorge because this section is not only a tyre shredder but lacks the scenery, specky camps and epic swimming spots.

From Derby, it's an easy daytrip to any of the gorges. One of my all-time favourite drives is up the Tunnel Creek Road, officially known as the Fairfield–Leopold Downs Road from the south. You can visit the magnificent Tunnel Creek and Geikie Gorge (Danggu) then turn onto the Gibb River Road and either keep exploring all the gorges or turn left and head over to Derby or Broome. Or the other way around starting from Derby, heading down the Tunnel Creek road and looping back to Broome or once hitting the highway again keep heading on to Fitzroy Crossing.

The truly adventurous can head north up the bone-rattling Kalumburu Road before turning left onto the Port Warrender Road and heading to the iconic Mitchell River National Park. The 172-kilometre drive can be challenging but is well worth the effort. Bushwalks, waterfalls, rock art, swimming, fishing, chopper tours – it's a veritable bush playground. For many, to reach the Mitchell Falls is a badge of honour representing the pinnacle of their four-wheel-driving lives.

Fuel and tyres

In case you misjudged how thirsty your fuel guzzler might get, are sick of burnt camp-oven meals or had your tyres slashed on the Wyndham end of the Gibb, there are two places that can help you out: Imintji Store and Mount Barnett Roadhouse. Both have takeaway food, fuel and coffee. But if you've limped in with tyre trouble or you're needing a minor repair, Imintji Store can help you get back on the road. The fact there's a busy, full-time tyre shop there is a solid indicator that the Gibb, especially the razor-sharp rock from Mount Barnett to Wyndham, is a tyre-slashing nightmare. If you're doing this leg, it's essential you carry a second spare.

KRISTY, DANNY AND MOLLY DO THE TELEGRAPH TRACK

When we were stranded at Fitzroy Crossing in the heart of Bunuba country in the Kimberley, I caught up with Kristy, Danny and Molly, a mum, dad and daughter trio. They'd come from Coolup, half an hour or so south-east of Mandurah  in Western Australia, and were travelling with a group of fellow four-wheel-drive vansters, trailer campers and motorhomers.

Danny proudly gave me a tour of his purpose-built motorhome. It was handmade from the chassis up, an all-in-one type with a mini apartment box bolted onto the back of a truck with a double bed, a single bed for their daughter, a kitchen, toilet, shower – the works. The upfront power plant was a 5-litre Cummins diesel with a roomy truck cab on top.

'It's my old work truck, an Isuzu NPS 300, four-wheel drive, six-tonner,' Danny told me. 'I used to run a mobile-mechanic business out of it.'

Danny's favourite addition was a massive freezer and an even bigger fridge that could accommodate a serious amount of beer. The whole thing was solar powered with a few hundred litres of water stored under the floor.

'I've worked hard most of my life, so I just wanted to travel,' Danny said. 'I got tied up with a young fellow I was working with, and two years ago he invited me to go to Cape York with this group of amazing people. We call ourselves the Carnage Crew, 'cause we see who can do the most damage on a trip. Now we're back here again, trying to do the Gibb River Road, but we've been rained in.'

Danny and Kristy loved travelling in a group. 'It's a great crew,' Danny said. 'Lots of camaraderie. We're all mechanics and auto-electricians – all sorts of stuff – so there's not a lot we can't sort out.'

'And why a truck-based motorhome rather than a van?' I asked.

'I'm always a bit different,' Danny replied. 'The others hate me because they'd be here for half an hour still setting up. I'll pull up and open the door, pull the steps out and that's it. It has its advantages that way, but if these guys pull up and unhook their cars, they can go for a daytrip and stuff like that. And its big, so we can't get into a lot of places. We had to replace half the side awnings, doors and toolboxes. They all smashed off on the last trip with the Carnage Crew.'

'So, you've done some pretty rough work in it?' I queried.

'We did a little bit of the old Telegraph Track in North Queensland where we could get in. That's where we lost all the awnings and mirrors. They're still sitting up there, somewhere.'

'The Telegraph Track was quite hair-raising,' Kristy said. 'On a couple of tracks I got out with a bottle of wine and walked. There was no way I was staying in. The truck was on two or three wheels at times, and I was like, "I'm not doing this, Danny." I had tears.'

'So you like more out-of-the-way, wild places?'

'The further away from civilisation, the better,' Danny said. 'Caravan parks are good for a good shower and a washing machine, but yeah, totally prefer off the grid. It's a great life.'

Watch Video: Oodnadatta Track Makers

The Oodnadatta Track

If you're looking for an alternative to a few days of bituminised tedium on the Stuart Highway to Alice Springs, this South Australian stretch of dirt is for you. There's no need for a fully fitted-out four-wheel drive loaded up with recovery gear – 'the Track' is perfect for outback-exploring newbies and seasoned travellers who just want a comfy cruise, especially those with plenty of time to check out the multitude of attractions. The track is well maintained and drivable all year round, *except* after rain. A sturdy vehicle with some ground clearance is advisable and carrying plenty of water is essential.

I've travelled this route many times and enjoyed every minute of it. I've made films here, including stories about the track-maintenance crew and the pilot who does air tours out of William Creek. But the most interesting was a film about the Marree Man, the largest ground drawing (or 'geoglyph') on earth, carved into the arid ground, its origins still shrouded in mystery.

From the south, the track officially begins at Marree and these days finishes at Marla on the Stuart Highway, a 614-kilometre journey in total. It's mostly dry, flat and treeless but boasts springs, sculpture parks, character-filled towns and inescapable reminders of its fascinating past.

The crumbling remains of the Farina post office, one of many ruins to be seen.

History

It's said the track is actually an ancient trading-and-travelling route taken by the original owners and inhabitants the Kuyani, Arabana and Arrernte people on the northern end.

It's hard to imagine how these groups survived in such an inhospitable environment, but the route follows a string of artesian springs that bubble to the surface, which must have provided sustenance to the nomads.

The springs also determined the route of the legendary Overland Telegraph connecting Australia to the rest of the world via Darwin and Java in 1872. The cable cut the speed of communication from months, via sailing ships, to a matter of hours, and has been described as Australia's 'greatest engineering feat' of the 19th century.

Six years later, construction commenced on a railway line from Port Augusta to Oodnadatta that became known as the Ghan Express. This was due to the predominantly Afghan cameleers that worked on its construction. The line reached Oodnadatta in 1891, then a three-year build from 1926 saw the first steam train arrive in Alice Springs in 1929. Now the Ghan goes all the way up to Darwin, but since 1980 it follows a route well to the west of the original alignment.

World War II saw the rail service greatly expanded to transport military vehicles and troops to Alice Springs. This required a good water supply for the thirsty steam engines, so demineralising water towers were built along the route to utilise the mineral-rich bore water. The giant cast-iron reservoirs still dot the landscape today.

Mutonia Sculpture Park at Alberrie creek is something to behold!

Springs, ruins and a bizarre sculpture park

Unlike many bone-rattling, endless dirt nightmares, the Oodnadatta Track is like a never-ending fun park, with interesting stopovers and things to check out along the way.

Marree has a great pub with basic accommodation and meals, and you can take a look at Tom Kruse's old Leyland Badger Truck, which sits out the front of the pub. Tom was a lesser-known movie star who featured in the 1954 BBC-produced film *Back of Beyond*. The iconic black-and-white film follows Tom and his offsider as they do the mail run from Marree to Birdsville in 1953, battling sandhills, breakdowns and sandstorms. It's a must-see!

Short side tracks will deliver you to mound springs, views of Kati Thanda-Lake Eyre, old rail sidings and sand dunes to play on. At William Creek, air charters are available to get an eagle's view of Painted Hills, Kati Thanda-Lake Eyre and the now only faintly visible Marree Man.

 Watch Video: Bush Pilot

North of William Creek is the Mutoid Waste Company's 'post-apocalyptic' sculpture park created by ex-car mechanic and artist Robin Cooke with permission from the traditional owners of the land. Made from discarded aeroplanes and recycled metal, and utilising existing human-made structures, the park is a self-funded anarchic playground and a must-see stopover. Where else are you going to see two aeroplanes painted up and sitting vertically on the ground? There are giant wind chimes and creations straight from the tangled mind of its creator.

The track continues on through Oodnadatta, once home to another artist, Adam Plate. Adam was a graduate from East Sydney Technical College but wasted no time moving on from art school to create the Pink Roadhouse with his wife, Lynnie, along with hundreds of signs erected along the track, all painted on bright-pink flour-drum lids. Adam was one of the inland's most colourful characters and liked to attract visitors to the area with his artworks emblazoned with 'Oodnadatta – Arsehole of the Earth'. The Pink Roadhouse is still there, but sadly Adam was killed in a vehicle accident in 2012, and Lynnie packed up and sold the ol' pink landmark.

The simplest of set ups.

Watch Video: Marree Man Mystery

Turn off and turn on to four-wheel-drive adventure

Today the track terminates as it turns on to the Stuart Highway at Marla Roadhouse, but adventurous four-wheel drivers can continue north-east to the therapeutic waters of Dalhousie Springs, a vast body of bubbling artesian water that sits between 38 and 43 degrees Celsius all year round. In peak season, you'll need to book a camp spot, as the place turns into a four-wheel-drive, camping and caravan car park.

From Dalhousie Springs you can head to the remote Mount Dare Hotel, and super adventurers with plenty of time and good suspension can head on to the old rail siding and now Aboriginal community of Finke.

From Finke you can head to Alice Springs along a route that follows the original Ghan railway line. Unless you want to experience the thrills and spills and thousands of camping spectators of the Finke Desert Race, avoid the place in early June.

Dad and daughter about to take on the road to hell.

The Savannah Way

As the name suggests, it's a way, not a standalone highway, track or road, as it's made up of a few different roads and highways joined together to link Cairns with Broome. The Savannah Way was created more as a marketing exercise by state and territory governments to lure travellers to our northern extremes. Most of the Way is bitumen and will take you through fabulous places in Northern Queensland, the Northern Territory and the Kimberley region of Western Australia.

I won't go into detail about the entire length of the 3700-kilometre scenic drive other than to say it's well worth doing and you will get a good overall picture of the northern regions of our continent.

View as you leave the Cairns hinterland.

From tropical and tourist-rich Cairns, it's lush hinterland, parched outposts and Northern Territory water attractions, then on through the rugged Kimberley to Broome. If you take it on you have definitely seen northern Australia and gained a badge of honour for doing it. For detailed information about the Way and the extensive variety of things you can see and do along its entire length, best head online.

But having done it recently with my daughter, I think it's way more helpful to describe the four-wheel-drive section from where the bitumen finishes at Normanton in Queensland and starts again at Mataranka in the Northern Territory. This part of the Way is for the strong-willed and strong chassis-ed, as it's not great for towing anything, let alone a caravan or trailer! That's something the state and territory tourist promoters don't want to promote.

TRAVELS WITH GINA

Cairns to Katherine, August 2022

Gina's favourite things, a bush camp, her HiLux and a cold beer,
near Kununurra, Western Australia.

My daughter, Gina, was born in Broome and, along with her four brothers, accompanied her mother and me on countless trips throughout the Kimberley and across the wilds of Australia. She's totally comfortable in the bush and loves a long drive, just like her dad. She knows the ropes when it comes to camping, cooking and being behind the wheel. She now has her very own HiLux four-wheel drive and thinks nothing of throwing in the swag and traversing the country from her home town in Broome to my place on the far south coast of New South Wales.

I love every second of our expeditions. We're a well-oiled travelling, swagging, tailgate-cooking duo. So, on a recent drive back to Broome, we went the long way to see what the Savannah Way was all about.

After cruising the bitumen river from resort town Cairns and through the ups and downs of some pretty cute towns, we made for one of our all-time favourite pubs in the heart of the Gulf Country: the Croydon Club Hotel. This gem of the outback ticks all the boxes for a genuine pub experience: icy beer, perfectly good tucker, dusty characters in droopy, sweat-stained Akubras and no-nonsense accommodation.

We arrived at the pub just in time to grab a schooner, bags our spot on the veranda and watch the setting sun over a plate of steak, chips and salad. This was our last swagless night before we headed west into the unknown dirt section of the Savannah Way.

A private collection of rusty legends, Croydon, Queensland.

In the morning, the town was ghostly quiet. The pub's neighbours had a paddock chockers with old trucks, Land Rovers, some classic yank tanks, mobile cranes and a row of legendary Blitz trucks that were probably the first vehicles to arrive at the remote outpost. I introduced myself to the proud owner of the rust collection and got a tour, met his wife and exchanged yarns. Turned out he was a master saddler as well.

THE BLITZ AND THE ROVER

After World War II, the army sold off their fleet of Blitz trucks. These virtually indestructible beasts were made in Canada and shipped to Commonwealth countries where the terrain called for a high-clearance, go-anywhere, solid and reliable truck.

The odd Blitz started to appear to supplement the existing use of horses and camels to get around the huge tracts of land or to run into town for supplies. They were fitted out with either Ford or Chevrolet motors, and

Series One Land Rover.

became ubiquitous throughout rural and remote Australia. Station owners and miners snapped them up, and they can still be seen scattered in far-flung rust yards right across the country.

Land Rovers were the vehicle of choice for Australian government employees like Walter MacDougall. He was an early missionary and later employed by the Emu Field atomic testing facility at Woomera. Prior to the first mainland atomic tests, he was charged with the inhumane and in retrospect outrageous task of removing Pitjantjatjara and Yankuntjatjara people from their lands in northern South Australia to a safer destination at Yalata further south. But his name became synonymous with his trusty old Land Rover and people had no trouble recalling it as the first car they ever saw. I know this from filming their eyewitness accounts of the atomic tests' black cloud, 30 years later to the day.

Just one of the classic buildings in this remote town.

Up the track, we entered the time warp that is Normanton. This olde-worlde outpost is fairly nondescript, but it is full of character and has plenty of things to check out, like the giant croc replica of a *real* one said to be the biggest ever caught. The whole place is uncanny and one of those towns that makes you wonder just why anyone would live here. But I'd say it has a tight and supportive bunch of locals who wouldn't be anywhere else.

Then it was on to the dirt, which wasn't too bad ... yet.

Before long we blew our first tyre. Luckily, we had a second spare and were not worried about repairing our first one, so we powered on. Dirty and dusty, we were especially looking forward to a wash and a freshen-up at the Leichhardt Falls up the road – so was half the vanning population of the north. We'd seen snaps and even a big roadside sign advertising the Leichhardt Falls cascading into a pool the size of a football field.

By the time we manoeuvred around the scores of parked vans and associated sunbathers we discovered the only thing falling at the Leichhardt Falls was fresh air and that the pool was a stretch of green slime. To be fair, it's a seasonal thing but, since it was dry, we got out of there, built a bridge and moved on.

Burketown was fairly forgettable – bar the unswimmable but colourful hot springs – so we pressed on west into the Gulf scrub country.

Scrub camp where I was nearly horned by a wild bull, near Doomadgee, Queensland.

After fuelling up at the Doomadgee Roadhouse we started to look for a camp spot. The dense scrub and herds of cattle didn't make finding our dream camp easy. As it was getting late, we headed down a station track and made do with an area cleared by the local bovine inhabitants, who seemed to have gone on dinner break. Then things got real. Gina had just laid out the swags and was getting a fire going as I was rustling a few things out of the tuckerbox when I heard a loud whisper: 'DAAAD!'

I swung around to be confronted by a massive Droughtmaster bull and his substantial harem. They were just 3 metres away and staring me down. I emitted my bravest and loudest bull-repelling 'Gowarrrn!' and waved my hat like a rodeo clown. It worked – slowly. The bull reluctantly snorted and turned his massive razor-tipped horns before plodding away into the scrub with his band of mooing devotees. As a precaution against having our heads squashed under a stampede of hoofs, we put the head ends of our swags under the car.

In the morning, I plugged the tyre puncture, which seemed to stop the air escaping, then we hit the cattle-infested dirt road to Hell's Gate.

Hell's Gate obviously got its name for being the gateway to outback *motoring* hell. The 330-kilometre stretch to Borroloola and over the border into the Northern Territory must have been created to road-test not only tyres, but shock absorbers, engine mounts – in fact, every movable part on a thing with wheels – and, more importantly, a motorist's endurance. It's a shocker!

Plugging tyres is just part of the fun.

PLUGGING TYRES

Once upon a time all tyres had tubes. Then in the mid–1950s tubes went the way of the Tassie tiger and disappeared, except for their ongoing use in split rims. So if you puncture your tubeless tyre it can be easily fixed with a rubber plug, like putting your finger in a dyke. A skinny strip of pliable rubber known as a plug is threaded through a small device that is a cross between a corkscrew and a large needle. Once you have located the hole push the needle holding the strip of rubber into the puncture hole then pull out again, leaving the rubber in the hole. Cut the rubber close to its neighbouring tread and bingo! If you have torn a huge hole or the puncture is in the wall of the tyre plugging will not work ... you will need a new tyre!

We blew our repaired second spare then plugged the spare, then plugged that twice more and limped into Borroloola sore, dusty and as shaken as a whisky sour. With no more spares and all faith in the plugs, we fuelled up for the last leg.

After a sublime stretch of bitumen, we turned off and headed north towards Roper Bar.

Out of the blue we were surprised to find the stunning Limmen National Park. There we took time out to do a little exploring of the bizarre rocky outcrops known as the Lost City.

The national park brought a break in the cattle infestation, so we started to look for a suitable camp. According to the map there were camping grounds by waterfalls and rivers dotted around but we unexpectedly came across a series of homemade signs directing us to a private cattle-station camping operation at Lorella Springs.

Limmen National Park, a maze of rock formations, Northern Territory.

By now we really had to find a spot to make camp, so we headed down the 20 kilometres or so to the Lorella Springs Wilderness Park. Turned out it was a privately owned and run tourist destination with every kind of fun thing you can do in the bush without getting lost, injured or destroying your home on wheels. Hand-painted signs directed us to springs, waterfalls, fishing spots, spring-fed thermal pools – the attractions were vast.

Apparently, the wilderness park is a well-known and much-loved piece of the planet that attracts four-wheel drivers from every direction. But since we visited, it appeared the owner had had to close due to excessive red tape, and the frolicking fun times in the bush might have fizzled out.

We camped by a hot spring creek at a clearing the size of the MCG, with fellow vanners and tent dwellers dotted about.

As evening approached, and with my dutiful daughter toiling away making dinner over a hot tailgate, I stretched out on my swag looking wistfully up into the heavens in wonder at Mother Nature's diamond-studded creation.

Then I noticed a moving set of more than 50 lights in the form of a massive sausage drifting across the sky. My jaw dropped.

'Gina! Check that out!' I yelled, pointing upwards.

Gina swung around.

'Oh my fucking god! What is it?!' she screamed.

The giant sausage continued on towards the horizon.

'Hey everyone, look at that!' Gina called out to the other campers. 'It's Santa's sleigh!'

Our neighbours must have thought we were on a bigger trip than the one to Broome and took no notice. We had no phone coverage to check whether it was a drone invasion, aliens or a formation of jets, and no more giant sausages drifted through the sky.

By morning, our last repaired tyre had let go some air, but we threw caution to the corrugations, pumped it up and headed off to Roper Bar.

Once again, the road was one long stretch of deep bulldust, corrugations and sharp rocks just perfect for slashing or puncturing our tyres, but they held together. Eventually we started to see handmade signs pointing out the various things available at the Roper Bar Park and Store. I was up for a steak sandwich and low-sugar ginger beer, and Gina was salivating in anticipation of a hamburger with the lot washed down with a cold can of lemon-flavoured mineral water. The tank was down to a quarter, so we also needed to fuel up.

Our tyres held together. We pulled up next to the diesel bowser and entered the ramshackle roadhouse on stilts. We both deserved a slap-up roadhouse lunch, so ordered our grease-dripping delectables with gusto.

'Sorry, we outta tucker,' the roadhouse-weary attendant replied.

There was stunned silence. 'Well, we'll just fill up with diesel then,' I said finally.

The Tourist-Unfriendly raised her eyes. 'No diesel, either,' she exclaimed with what sounded suspiciously like joy.

'Farrrrk' was our joint response. A quarter tank of diesel for 183 kilometres! We had little choice but to take it on – without any more spare tyres!

After buying two deformed icy poles we set off to meet our fate.

We didn't dare get over 70 kilometres per hour. Forty kilometres out of Mataranka on the Stuart Highway the dirt finally gave way to a thin strip of bitumen. We continued to gingerly cruise along, dropping to 50 kilometres per hour as, in unison, we watched the needle on the fuel gauge drop. It reached the E, then the second prong of the E, then the third. Now we were in below-empty land. Signs for the Mataranka hot springs, motels and cold beer at the pub began to appear. It looked like we might just make it.

I checked for coverage on the mobile, but there was nothing – strange. We gently turned right off the highway into Mataranka and pulled up next to the first bowser we saw.

'No internet – cash only.'

There were cardboard signs on every bowser.

Not only did we have to find cash in the car somewhere, but we still couldn't solve the mystery of the cosmic sausage we'd seen the night before.

After a frenzied scramble through the cab and mining operations under the seats, glovebox, doors and floor mats, we gathered

$14.25. We prayed to the HiLux fairies and gods of the white lines that this would be enough to get us to Katherine. Which it did – just.

Ensconced in a cosy cabin in a caravan park with pool and restaurant, we could put the corrugations, dirt, near-stranding, tyre-fixing dramas behind us. There was just one matter left to attend to: the cosmic sausage.

A Google search revealed it was an Elon Musk Starlink satellite cluster on its way to dispersing 53 mini-satellites to the heavens, another master stroke of technological genius and far more important than sending a grader to smooth the Savannah Way.

9

YOU'RE READY AND SET TO GO BUSH

There is no vaccine that will give us immunity to the unforeseen dramas and difficulties we face on our journey from the womb to the great beyond.

No medicine will cure the world of all its wars and injustices. It may be considered escapist, but sometimes the call for self-preservation or an escape hatch from the day-to-day is deafening, and it's simply time to hit the road and go bush. As someone who has been dealt their fair share of blows and adversity, I've found the bush to be a source of constant comfort and a touchstone to remind me that, as living beings, we are part of nature itself. To engage with the natural world is to appreciate something way bigger than us; treat it kindly and the rewards are immeasurable. Going bush can take you out of your comfort zone and require of you a certain amount of making do and going back to basics. A road trip will broaden your horizons and give you a window into just what's going on out there while engaging with others doing the same thing.

Being asked to write this book made me question … what makes my experience so special that others might want to read about it? As a boy growing up in industrial Wollongong I would never have dreamt my life would be so enriched by so many people, places and experiences. For me, to have a life as a filmmaker in remote Australia and be informed by its original inhabitants was a gift that was extra special. It was really something to be raised by a loving family who passed on their love of the bush to me; that I then instilled the same appreciation to my own family has been one of my greatest and most satisfying achievements.

The Batty gang, Finke River, Northern Territory.

So, I hope these pages have enlightened and in turn motivated you to get out and enjoy what this huge island has on offer. My advice tips and yarns are all written from my personal experiences.

As they say, 'Your next big adventure starts with the first step.'

Getting organised to exit the driveway can be daunting and hard on the wallet, but once out on the open road, a week or two into your road trip or making camp you will be glad you prepared for whatever might come your way. Take time to appreciate nature's wonders, explore country towns and their history, yarn with some locals or sit by a campfire with your beloved.

Happy camping.

10

The perfect dinner camp, Carmila Beach, Queensland.

CAMP KITCHEN FAVOURITES

Good food and plenty of it has been my recipe for success when it comes to catering on film shoots in the bush or on countless camping trips with my family. I always seem to end up being the cooky and I've never had one single complaint … Well, there *was* the iffy fish stew. Over the decades I've developed a repertoire of camp-kitchen favourites. Some recipes require things out of an esky or car fridge while other dishes are either freshly caught or from non-perishables. If you don't have all the ingredients, just go with what you've got or get creative. Quantities are 'whatever you reckon will feed your crew'.

Bluebone fish on coals

Bluebone fish, or whatever you can catch

Salt and pepper

Lemon juice

- Catch bluebone or other ocean fare. Gut and degill the fish, leaving the head and scales on.
- Light a fire with plenty of small sticks to make coals.
- Reduce the fire to a bed of red–hot coals.
- Place the fish on the coals and cook until the flesh is soft.
- Remove the fish from the coals and peel back the skin and scales.
- Add salt, pepper and lemon juice.
- Eat with your fingers.

Tuna puttanesca

Dried bow-tie pasta

Olive oil

Garlic, sliced

Tin of tuna

Olives, pitted

Capers

Chilli flakes

Cherry tomatoes, halved

- Heat enough water in a pot or billy to cook the pasta. When the water is boiling, add bow-tie pasta and cook according to packet instructions.
- In a pan or camp oven, lightly fry chopped garlic in olive oil.
- Drain and add the tin of tuna to the garlic along with the olives, capers and chilli flakes. Stir lightly and cook for a few minutes.
- Drain pasta and add to cooked ingredients.
- Add a dash more olive oil, stir and cook for 2 minutes.
- Add halved cherry tomatoes and cook a further 2 minutes, until tomatoes are soft.
- Serve with parmesan cheese and cracked pepper (the dish should already be salty enough).

Abalone

Abalone

Flour

Olive oil

Salad ingredients such as lettuce, onion and tinned beetroot, for

serving

- Dive for or acquire fresh legal abalone (laws vary from state to state).
- Remove the meat from the shell and cut out the guts.
- Pound the meat once or twice with a rock until it softens but is still intact.
- Cut the meat lengthways into 0.5 centimetre strips and toss in flour.
- Fry in olive oil for 30–60 seconds.
- Serve with tinned beetroot and lettuce salad.

Coconut dahl and veg

Packet/s of coconut dahl (available from the supermarket)

Mixed vegetables, chopped

- Heat the coconut dahl in a pot.
- Add the chopped vegetables.
- Cook until the veggies are tender.

Chicken stir fry

Chicken thighs

Olive oil

Whole star anise

Mixed vegetables (for example, carrot, cabbage, celery, zucchini), chopped

Chicken or vegetable stock (If powdered or cubed, dissolve in ½ cup water

Rice for serving

- Cut chicken thighs into three or four pieces.
- Sauté in olive oil until just cooked.
- Add whole star anise.
- Add chopped vegetables.
- Add stock and toss until veggies are tender.
- Serve with rice.

Sausage curry with salsa

<u>Curry</u>

Sausages (fat sausages from the butcher are best, but any will do)

Olive oil

Onions, sliced

Carrots, sliced

Curry powder

Sultanas

Teaspoon or so of cornflour

Rice for serving

- Boil the sausages until cooked. Drain and cut them into 4-centimetre chunks.
- Oil a pan and fry the sliced onions and carrots.
- Add the sausage chunks, curry powder, sultanas and around a teaspoon of corn flour.

<u>Salsa</u>

Red onion, finely chopped

Tomatoes, chopped

Cucumber, chopped

Olive oil

Salt and cracked pepper

- Mix the chopped onion, tomatoes and cucumber.
- Add a little olive oil, salt and cracked pepper and mix.
- Serve curry and salsa with cooked brown basmati rice.

Roast chicken and vegetables

Whole chicken, fresh or thawed

Onion, quartered

Lemon, quartered

Salt and cracked pepper

Lemon juice

Olive oil

Potatoes, sweet potato, carrots, more onion, pumpkin, cut into chunks

- Make a decent fire.
- Stuff the chicken with the quarters of onion and the quartered lemon.
- Place the chicken breast up in an oiled camp oven.
- Season chicken with salt, cracked pepper, lemon juice and olive oil.

- Place the chunks of potatoes, sweet potato, carrots, onion and pumpkin around the chicken.
- Put the lid on the camp oven and place it on a bed of hot coals away from the flame.
- Cook for 40–60 minutes, checking every 20 minutes.
- Replenish the hot coals if or as necessary.

Lamb stew

Any cut of lamb, or lamb chops
Olive oil
Carrots, chopped
Potatoes, chopped
Fresh or tinned tomatoes, chopped
Frozen, dried or canned peas
Rice or buttered bread for serving

- Cube the lamb and sauté it in a little olive oil until tender.
- Add the chopped carrots and potatoes and cook for 5 minutes.
- Add the tomatoes and cook for 20–30 minutes
- Add the frozen, dried or canned peas and cook for 5 minutes.
- Serve with rice or buttered bread.

Bacon and zucchini pasta

Dried bow-tie pasta

Olive oil

Bacon, chopped

Garlic, chopped

Zucchini, chopped

Cherry tomatoes, halved

Parmesan cheese for serving

- Boil a pot or billy of water and add the bow-tie pasta.
- In a camp oven, sauté the bacon and garlic in a little olive oil.
- Add the zucchini and cook until tender.
- Add the tomatoes and cook for 3 minutes or until soft.
- Drain the pasta and return to the pot.
- Add to the pasta the bacon, garlic, zucchini and tomato mix, a splash of olive oil and salt and cracked pepper.
- Mix over the heat for 2 minutes.
- Serve with parmesan cheese.

Thai beef salad

Salad

Thick beef steak or other cut of beef

Cucumber, sliced

Cherry tomatoes, halved

Cos lettuce, chopped

Red onion, sliced

Mint

Coriander

Thai basil

Peanuts, chopped

Dressing

Lime juice

Garlic, minced

Fish sauce

Sesame oil

Soy sauce

Sugar

- Either barbecue (if you're cooking a thick beef steak) or bake (for a larger cut of beef) until the meat is still rare in the centre. Let cool.
- In a bowl, add cucumber, cherry tomatoes, cos lettuce, red onion, herbs and peanuts.
- For the dressing, combine all ingredients.
- Slice the beef into thin strips, mix it into the salad, add the dressing and stir again.
- Serve with rice.

Vietnamese chicken salad

<u>Salad</u>

Whole chicken or chicken breasts

Carrots, thinly sliced

Cucumber, thinly sliced

Cos lettuce or cabbage, sliced

Cherry tomatoes, halved

Mint

Coriander

Roasted peanuts, chopped

<u>Dressing</u>

Lime juice

Fish sauce

Sugar

- In a pot or billy, bring the chicken to the boil for 12 minutes then let it sit in water for 10 minutes more.
- Remove the chicken from the pot and let cool.
- Shred the chicken meat with your fingers.
- Combine the carrot, cucumber, cos lettuce or cabbage, cherry tomatoes and herbs.
- For the dressing, combine all ingredients.
- Mix the shredded chicken with the salad and the dressing. Sprinkle with peanuts and serve with rice.

Muesli porridge

Water

Milk

Muesli

Banana, sliced

Honey

Butter

Brown sugar (optional)

- Combine a mix of half-water and half-milk with muesli and steep overnight or for at least 30 minutes.
- Cook the mix in a pot with the banana and honey, adding more milk or water if needed.
- Serve with warm milk, a dab of butter and brown sugar.

Roast veggies

Veggies such as potatoes, pumpkin, carrots, sweet potato, fennel, and onion, cut into large chunks

Whole garlic cloves

Olive oil

Cracked pepper

- Toss the veggies in olive oil, salt and cracked pepper.
- Place the veggies in a camp oven, put the lid on and set it on coals for one hour or until cooked.
- Serve with peas or other steamed greens.

Curried fish steaks

Onions, sliced

Garlic, chopped

Ginger, chopped

Curry paste (packet or tin)

OR

Fresh curry herbs and spices

Can of coconut milk

Frozen or fresh fish steaks

- Place the onions, garlic and ginger into a camp oven or frying pan
- Add the curry paste or fresh curry herbs and spices.
- Stir in the can of coconut milk and cook for 5 minutes.
- Add fresh or frozen mackerel, tuna or swordfish steaks (or any other kind of firm-fish steak) and fold into the coconut mix.
- Put the lid on the camp oven or pan and cook until the fish is tender – about 15 minutes max.
- Serve with rice and salsa (for salsa recipe, see page 298).

T-bone and veggies in foil

Foil for wrapping

Olive oil

Onions, sliced

T-bone steak

Capsicum, sliced

Zucchinis, cut in strips

Tomatoes, sliced

- Get a decent-sized cooking fire going.
- Cut off a 50-centimetre length of foil and pour some olive oil onto it.
- On the foil, lay out a thick bed of sliced onions about the size of the steak.
- Place the steak on top of the onions.
- Place the capsicum, zucchini and tomato slices on top of the steak.

- Fold up the sides of the foil over the steak, then the ends, to create a parcel.
- Place the foil parcel on top of the coals and cook for 20–30 minutes. Don't cover the parcel with coals.

Cabbage and tuna

Garlic, chopped

Cabbage, chopped

Large can of tuna (in oil or spring water)

- Fry the garlic and cabbage until well cooked.
- Stir in the tuna.
- Serve with rice.

Extras

Short films, documentaries and YouTube channels made by the author.

 Ringers of the Kimberley

 Kimberley Bull Buggies

 Bush Mechanics – episode one – Motorcar Ngutju

 Kimberley Rock Art

 Larapinta Trail Makers

 Rodeo Road

 Sisters Pearls and Mission Girls

 Stumpy Brown – First Contact

Black As YouTube Channel

 Rebel Films YouTube Channel

Image Credits

All images courtesy of the author with the exception of: Adobe Stock – 53, 61–62, 97, 109; Shutterstock – title page, chapter opener rust pattern and title plates, 97; Wikimedia Commons 54

In Appreciation ...

This book would not have happened without the support of publisher Georgia Frances King, who provided ute loads of encouragement to write and support me through some challenging times including the loss of my dear old mum and a devastating bushfire at my property.

A big thanks to my partner Jen McMahon who was a constant sounding board of my thoughts and meanderings. My children Jack, Franque, Nick and especially Gina who was my travelling companion and star of many of the photos that appear in this book. Also thanks to their mother Alison who supported me in my early filmmaking and family adventures.

A special shout out to Narelle Perroux and Carol Jefferies, who were my fabulous travelling companions on a research trip around the country.

I owe much of this book, a fair chunk of my life's education and many an adventure to my Aboriginal friends, companions and collaborators, especially Francis Jupurrurla Kelly and the *Black As* boys, Chico, Dino, Jerome and Joe.

To all I've shared long drives, campfires, raising children, fun times and sad times, thanks a million, see you out there.